STUDIES IN EARLY MEI

Pagan Goddesses in the Early Germanic World

Eostre, Hreda and the Cult of Matrons

Philip A. Shaw

Bristol Classical Press

First published in 2011 by
Bristol Classical Press
an imprint of
Bloomsbury Academic
Bloomsbury Publishing Plc
50 Bedford Square
London WC1B 3DP

CIP records for this book are available from the
British Library and the Library of Congress

ISBN 978-0-7156-3797-5

Typeset by Ray Davies
Printed and bound in Great Britain by
CPI Antony Rowe, Chippenham and Eastbourne

www.bloomsburyacademic.com

Contents

parentibus meis

Acknowledgements

This book was completed during a research leave from the School of English Literature, Language and Linguistics at the University of Sheffield, for which I am very grateful. I would particularly like to thank Rebecca Rushforth and Richard Corradini: the former for her patient and speedy responses to peculiar queries about Anglo-Saxon calendars, the latter for his help with early manuscripts of *De Temporum Ratione*. I am also grateful to the libraries I have used in the course of my researches: Western Bank Library, University of Sheffield; the Brotherton Library, University of Leeds; and the British Library. I am especially grateful to the staff of the Bibliothèque nationale de France, and the library of the Institut de Recherche et d'Histoire des Textes, who were unfailingly helpful as I worked my way through a large number of manuscripts and microfilms. Chapter 4 developed out of a paper given at the International Medieval Congress in Leeds in July 2007: I am grateful to the other session participants, and the audience of this paper, for their questions and suggestions. I am also grateful to the University of Sheffield's Medieval Discussion Group, with whom I had fruitful discussions of aspects of the material discussed in this chapter. Siân Prosser, Chris Walton, Cheryl Clay and Alaric Hall kindly read drafts of the text and made many useful suggestions. I am very grateful to Ian Wood, the editor of this series, and Deborah Blake at Bristol Classical Press, for their enthusiastic help with this project, and I owe Deborah special thanks for her patience in dealing with all the peculiar characters and strange illustrations involved. Naturally I alone am responsible for any faults in the finished product.

1

Introduction
The Footprint of Pre-Christian Worship

This book is intended to fulfil a number of roles: a brief introduction to philological methods for historians, a (necessarily partial) analysis of the nature of pre-Christian religious life in Anglo-Saxon England, but also a rescue. Not only does it seek to rescue a pair of goddesses in distress, Eostre and Hreda, from being considered 'an etymological fancy' (Page 1995: 125) and relegated to a series of notes on the unlikelihood of their existence – it also seeks to rescue the Venerable Bede himself from the charge of having invented these pre-Christian deities. Whatever we may think of Bede's overall portrayal of the pre-Christian past of the English, I would argue that there is sufficient evidence to suggest that *Eostre* and *Hreda* are plausible names for Anglo-Saxon pre-Christian goddesses – and, moreover, names that give us some important clues to the ways in which social and religious life intersected in early Anglo-Saxon society.

Pre-Christian religion in the early Middle Ages

One of the central social and political developments of the early Middle Ages was the spread of Christianity among the Germanic-speaking peoples. This complex of changes profoundly affected the orientation of northwestern European societies in relation to the Mediterranean world, and laid the foundation for long-lasting political and social patterns, whose echoes can still be observed today. But we should not forget that these changes were fundamentally religious, and that they operated not upon a blank slate, but upon pre-existing religious situations whose outlines we can discern only with difficulty. These situations form the subject of this book.

There have been many attempts to write histories of Germanic paganisms: there are at least four books entitled *Altgermanische Religionsgeschichte* (literally 'old Germanic religion's history'; Meyer 1910; Helm 1913-53; Clemen 1934; De Vries 1956-57). This is not another such book. Indeed, I remain to be convinced that a satisfactory *Altgermanische Religionsgeschichte* can ever be written. Part of the problem is the term 'Germanic': much has been written about the usefulness or otherwise of this term as an ethnic identification, and some dark episodes in our recent past have been fuelled in part by ideas of a homogenous and historically-defined Germanic race. Much remains to be discovered about the various ways in which 'Germanic' and related terms have been employed – both by those who believed themselves to be Germanic, and by those who did not – over the last two thousand years or so. But these questions are not central to our purpose here. As the arguments advanced in what follows revolve principally around the ways in which linguistic evidence can be employed in historical reconstruction of pre-Christian religious life, I will use a far less problematic definition of the term 'Germanic'. For the purposes of this book, 'Germanic' refers to the Germanic languages, and when I refer to Germanic individuals, groups or deities, I am making no claims about race or ethnicity – only language. Thus a Germanic individual is one who speaks a Germanic language as a first language, and a Germanic group is a group of such individuals.

A Germanic deity is a slightly more slippery concept, however. As we shall see, there existed deities whose names were simply derived from Germanic words, by Germanic speakers; but there were also deities whose names were linguistic hybrids of a Celtic and a Germanic language, or of Latin and a Germanic language. We also have evidence for deities with both a Latin and a Germanic name or epithet. And this is before we even begin to consider whether those who worshipped a particular deity were themselves Germanic. In what follows, I will therefore refer to deities as Germanic in cases where their names are probably composed entirely of linguistically Germanic elements, but will use the term Romano-Germanic to refer to deities whose names represent mixed Germanic-Latin constructions. Votive inscriptions in Latin in which a Germanic deity-name features will also be termed Romano-Germanic. These terms are not intended to indicate the linguistic or ethnic affiliations of a deity's worshippers.

Nevertheless, one of our central concerns here will be the ways in which pre-Christian deities related to group identities in the early Middle Ages. Problems of language and of socio-political and ethnic identifiers are obviously important in dealing with such issues: being able to distinguish clearly between the linguistic characteristics of a deity's name and the social, political and religious characteristics of their worship is therefore more than simple quibbling. Indeed, I will insist below on the specificity of the deities discussed, and will argue that the study of pre-Christian deities more broadly requires just such an eye for the detail and the low-level patterns of their cults. This, then, represents the other major objection to the production of a monolithic *Altgermanische Religionsgeschichte*: there are, in my view, multiple histories of Germanic paganisms, which turn around numerous different cults and deities. The pre-Christian religious lives of Germanic-speaking peoples were various, and socially and politically contingent. To reduce them to a unified history tends to obscure (even if it does not seek to do so) their heterogeneity and their geographical and chronological specificity. Studying Germanic deities and their cults is, I suggest, eminently worth doing; but assuming that there was ever such a thing as 'Germanic paganism', and seeking to study it, is, I fear, to look for a homogeneous religious system that never really existed. The terms 'pre-Christian' and 'pagan' (or 'paganism') appear frequently in what follows, as convenient ways to refer to religious beliefs that stand outside the major world religions – but it should be borne in mind that the societies under examination here would probably not have recognised themselves as 'pagan', and that 'paganism' need not always stand chronologically before Christianity.

The footprint of a pre-Christian cult

The purpose of this book is not simply to argue against homogenising approaches to pre-Christian religious life: it is also intended to offer some models for working with the (often sparse) evidence for individual cults. The deities most frequently discussed, by modern scholars and medieval authors, do not feature here. The gods Thor, Odin, Frey and Tyr, to give them the Anglicised versions of their Old Norse names (*Þórr*, *Óðinn*, *Freyr*, *Týr*), are the subject of mythological narratives in Old Norse sources such as the *Prose Edda*. The goddesses Frigg and Freyja also feature in these narratives, and a number of other deities are named less frequently in Old Norse materials. The centrality of these deities – whom we can, for convenience, term the 'great gods' – in Old Norse mythological narrative has tended to promote a focus on these deities as central to pre-Christian religious life across most if not all of the Germanic-speaking peoples. Thus DuBois, for instance, in his thoughtful study of Scandinavian religious life, recognises the local and even personal specificities of deities' cults in Scandinavia (DuBois 1999: 46-61), yet unquestioningly accepts that Odin and Thor were pan-Germanic deities (DuBois 1999: 57). Such perspectives tend to predispose us to seeing the great gods in contexts where we have no particular evidence for their presence. For instance, Gannon (2003: 77-8) seeks to relate the image of a bird on an early Anglo-Saxon series of coins to 'Woden's raven', implicitly drawing on Old Norse descriptions of Odin as accompanied by two ravens. This identification draws on (and implies) the idea that Odin/Woden is a pan-Germanic deity, always and everywhere the same in Germanic societies. Yet while texts produced in Anglo-Saxon England do mention Woden, they never link him with ravens, and they offer little evidence for his characteristics as an object of pre-Christian cult. How similar any Anglo-Saxon cult of Woden was to the cult of Odin in Scandinavia is not an easy question to answer, and it is, I would suggest, a question that cannot simply be dismissed in favour of an assumption that Odin's characteristics must also have been Woden's characteristics, and *vice versa*.

A tendency to see the great gods where they need not be could distort our overall understanding of pre-Christian religious life among the Germanic-speaking peoples. At the same time, a failure to recognise the wealth of deities beyond the great gods can also create distortions, and it is this aspect of the debate that is the particular focus of this book. I hope that the issues raised here may impact on the way scholars deal with the great gods, but I will not discuss these deities: that would require a rather longer book. Instead, the discussions that follow will centre around a pair of case studies of somewhat less visible deities, attempting to provide at least a partial picture of some of the ways in which the less visible cults of deities not among the great gods may have operated. In examining these deities, we will concern ourselves principally with what one might loosely term their 'footprint': that is, both the surviving evidence for them, and what that evidence tells us about the geographical, socio-political, linguistic, ethnic and chronological distributions of their cults. The surviving evidence is, of course, fragmentary and partial, and we can reasonably expect many aspects of the cults of pre-Christian deities (if not entire cults, in some cases) to have been ephemeral. But, like a set of footprints, the sparse evidence available to us can, if carefully analysed, tell us something about the size and impact of a deity, where they travelled, and when.

Evidence bases: how do we know about pre-Christian deities at all?

The sparseness of evidence for pre-Christian deities necessitates very careful consideration of the methodologies and assumptions brought to bear on the evidence, and the nature of the evidence itself. This book makes use of a body of evidence that has not received sustained scrutiny by medievalists: the votive inscriptions to Germanic, Romano-Germanic and Celto-Germanic deities produced in the late Roman period, from the first century AD through to the fourth. This corpus is discussed in greater detail in Chapter 3, so we need not dwell on it here. The problems of such evidence – produced earlier than the available early medieval evidence, and in rather different socio-political circumstances – are clearly substantial; but it also offers a very useful way of checking the evidence provided by early medieval authors. These authors are usually Christians, who naturally regard pre-Christian religious life with various preconceptions and biases. The votive inscriptions, as we shall see, have the benefit of allowing us a more direct view of the religious life of those who actually worshipped pagan deities. But this is not to say that this is an unproblematic view, given the fact that such inscriptions are originally a Roman practice, carried out using Roman artistic techniques. Nevertheless, the intersections and the disjunctions of indirect evidence produced in very different environments may well offer us useful opportunities for cross-checking the evidence with which medieval specialists are more familiar.

A word is necessary here about the early medieval sources of evidence as well. The case studies presented here focus on two deities mentioned by Bede in his *De Temporum Ratione* ('On the Reckoning of Time'). Evidence will also be drawn from a number of other texts, some of them in Old English and some in other Germanic dialects. Detailed discussion of the individual sources used will be introduced as necessary in each chapter, but we should note at the outset the literary character of many of these sources. I do not intend the word 'literary' here as a synonym for 'inaccurate' or 'untrustworthy': the point is that these sources are the products of high level intellectual endeavour, and should be understood within the intellectual climate of the monastic networks and royal courts in which they were created and disseminated. I am well aware that other sorts of evidence exist, particularly in the form of place-names and archaeological data. While the former will be discussed in some detail where appropriate, archaeological data of early medieval date do not figure greatly in the discussions. The problems and possibilities of such data are of a rather different kind from those discussed below, and it is often difficult to establish convincing identifications of archaeological materials with named deities. As a non-archaeologist, however, I should be wary of making large claims about archaeological evidence, and I will be glad to be corrected on this point if the evidence allows.

Language and history

The other major source of evidence here is essentially linguistic. The names of the deities themselves are words, and like other words, they can be subjected to various forms of linguistic analysis. The very considerable possibilities of applying such linguistic evidence in disentangling broader historical problems has been demonstrated by D.H. Green in various publications, among which his masterly book *Language and History in the Early Germanic World* (2000) is especially noteworthy. This slim volume cannot begin to match the scope and depth of Green's work, but it will attempt to present the workings of a few important linguistic arguments in as plain and comprehensible a way as possible, noting not only the results of the analyses, but also the methodological considerations involved in their application. I hope that this will demonstrate once again the possibilities of such approaches, as well as presenting some clear models for working in this area. This cannot, however, function as a handbook of historical linguistics, and in seeking to foster interdisciplinary research in the area, we should be considering team-based work across history, archaeology and language studies, and debates across these disciplines.

1. Introduction: The Footprint of Pre-Christian Worship

The need for such an approach is underlined by some of the misuses of linguistic evidence prevalent in work in this area. For example, Anthony Birley's fascinating account of the life of the Vindolanda garrison is slightly marred by a rather cavalier approach to linguistic evidence. His treatment of the *dibus veteribus* is worth quoting at length as an example of most of the common pitfalls:

> There are more than a dozen variant spellings of the deity. A plural form, *Veteribus* or *dibus veteribus*, seems to betray non-Latin origin, including *Hveteribus*, *Hvitiribus* in the plural, *Vetiri*, *Vetri*, *Vitiri*, *Hveteri*, *Hvitri*, *Vheteri* in the singular. These spellings, especially with *Hv-* or *Vh-*, show that the name could not readily be expressed in the Latin alphabet. This may be an ancient local spirit, ill-defined as to number (and even sex: two examples honour the *Vitires* as female), or perhaps originally a Germanic import – brought by the Batavians or Tungrians? Odin or Woden had the epithet *vithrir*, god of 'weather', no bad presiding spirit for the northern borderlands. Otherwise, the name might be connected with Old Nordic *hvitr*, 'white' or 'shining', or *hvethr-ung*, 'son of a giantess', applied to Loki, the equivalent of Vulcan. (Birley 2002: 163)

While Birley is right to note that the range of spellings employed in these inscriptions probably indicates difficulties in representing the name using the Latin alphabet, little else in this passage bears detailed scrutiny. To claim that 'Odin or Woden had the epithet *vithrir*' is to collapse a complex body of evidence in misleading ways: Odin does indeed have a by-name *Viðrir* in Old Norse poetry (see, for instance, *Lokasenna* stanza 26 and *Helgakviða Hundingsbana I* stanza 13; Larrington 1996: 89 and 116), but there is no evidence that an English equivalent of this by-name was ever applied to the Anglo-Saxon figure Woden. Nor would we necessarily be justified in regarding Odin and Woden as straightforward equivalents, or in assuming that their cults were identical in Anglo-Saxon and Scandinavian societies – even if we accept that their names are linguistically cognate. A similar problem arises with the identification of Loki as 'the equivalent of Vulcan', as we have no clear evidence for the currency of this equivalence in pre-Christian contexts.

The range of possible etymological identifications that Birley makes also raises questions. There is no discussion of the relative merits of identifications with *Viðrir*, *hvítr* or *hveðrung*, and Birley does not even state a preference for one of them. Indeed, he begins the next paragraph with yet another possible etymology: 'the "Old God(s)" suggests conservatism or reaction in the face of new religions' (Birley 2002: 164). This contradicts his previous discussion, suggesting an identification of *veteribus* with the dative plural form of the Latin adjective *vetus* ('old'). This is entirely satisfactory as a reading for forms beginning *v-*, but it does not account for the *vh-* and *hv-* forms. The latter forms are likely to reflect the origins of the term, as it is unlikely that one would accidentally add <h> to this word, but quite likely that some individuals would have omitted <h> on the basis that the forms without this letter resemble a meaningful Latin word. We might, then, suppose that some individuals re-interpreted these deities as 'the old god(s)', but we still have to account for the *vh-/hv-* forms in some other way.

The lack of discussion of the Old Norse terms proposed as possible relatives of this name is the most troubling aspect of this discussion. It appears that Birley has simply looked for words in Old Norse that appear similar to the forms in these inscriptions, without giving any thought to the phonological plausibility of his identifications. Given the point made above about the priority of forms with <h>, and the fact that these forms prompted Birley's identification of the name as of non-Latin origin in the first place, we can rule out the identification with *Viðrir*, as this by-name lacks initial <h>. Birley's other options, *hvítr* and *hveðrung*, are, therefore, linguistically more satisfactory, and might repay closer scrutiny. Of the two, *hvítr* is the more obvious candidate, as *hveðrung* is not certainly attested outside Old Norse, whereas relatives of *hvítr* (such as English *white*) exist right across the Germanic language family (Kluge and Seebold 2002: under *weiß*).[1]

If we are to avoid the pitfalls Birley has encountered, we must be careful in the way that we treat linguistic evidence. But our caution must not take the form of unreflective scepticism: we need to understand the possibilities as well as the limitations of linguistic evidence, and we need to have a basic grasp of the ways in which linguistic patterns can help us to understand the lives of the speakers of a given language. The next chapter addresses the basic models and methods that we need to be aware of, while Chapter 3 considers the evidence of Romano-Germanic inscriptions for the nature of Germanic pre-Christian religious life. This evidence, together with the linguistic methods, forms the basis for the detailed investigations of the goddesses Eostre and Hreda in Chapters 4 and 5.

2

Linguistic Models and Methods

This chapter is intended as a brief orientation to the linguistic methods that underpin some of the arguments put forward in the chapters that follow. It is intended to help non-specialists understand the bases on which these arguments are made, and the specialist terminology employed. Key linguistic terms that recur in subsequent chapters are therefore indicated in **bold**, as an aid to the reader. Of course, anyone with an understanding of the basics of word formation, phonology and comparative reconstruction should skip this chapter.

The building blocks of words

The words in a language (its **lexis**, or **vocabulary**) are each made up of a number of elements. At the simple level, a word is a sequence of sounds. In written form (at least in languages like English) it is a sequence of letters (or **graphs**). As anyone who has learnt to read and write English knows, however, there is not always a simple one-to-one relationship between sounds and graphs: for instance, the **graph** <c> (note that the use of angle brackets is standard practice when transcribing **graphs**, as opposed to sounds) represents completely different sounds in *cat* and *ace*. There are good historical reasons for this mismatch, but they do not concern us here. What is important for us to bear in mind is that there seems to have been a rather closer match between individual sounds and individual graphs in the spelling systems (or **orthographies**) of early Germanic languages such as Old English, Old High German and Old Norse.

The sounds of a language are circumscribed by two basic factors: one is the (really quite large) range of sounds that can be produced by the human vocal tract; the other is what the speakers of a language recognise as the sounds belonging to the language. It is the latter factor that matters in studying the history of a language and the people who spoke it. A number of jokes rely on the confusions that arise between native and non-native speakers of a language. A well-known example is the series of unfortunate miscommunications involving an Italian gentleman visiting an hotel in an English-speaking country, which culminates in the receptionist wishing him farewell with the somewhat improbable phrase 'peace on you', to which he replies 'piss on you too!'. Someone whose first language is English can readily distinguish between *peace* and *piss*, because they recognise the vowel sounds of these words as two different sounds: in Italian, however, there is only one sound that approximates to these vowels. We call the individual sounds distinguished by speakers of a language **phonemes**: in English, there are two different phonemes, a longer one in *peace* and a shorter one in *piss* (and there are other small differences in the pronunciation too), whereas in Italian there is a single phoneme (generally like a shorter version of the sound in *peace*).

We represent phonemes using the International Phonetic Alphabet, placing the symbols between slashes. Thus we could represent *peace* as /piːs/ and *piss* as /pɪs/. The symbol like a colon indicates that the vowel preceding it is long; otherwise the vowel is short. The two different symbols employed (/i/ and /ɪ/) indicate the slightly different pronunciations of the two phonemes. It is sometimes useful to specify whether a sound comes at the beginning of a word (as /p/ does in *peace*), or at the end of a word (/s/ in *peace*). We would term /p/ the **initial** sound of *peace* and /s/ the **final** sound (or we could talk about these sounds appearing **initially** or **finally** in the word). Any sounds which are not **initial** or **final** can be termed **medial**. In the case of *peace* /iː/ is the only medial sound.

Any given language will have a limited number of **phonemes**. In Old English and its Germanic relatives, the phonemes can be divided, broadly speaking, into vowels and consonants. I will not discuss consonants in detail here, but vowels are important to the arguments rehearsed in later chapters, so I will briefly outline the Old English vowel system. There are several factors that influence exactly how a vowel sounds, but the ones that we are concerned with are the position of the tongue in the mouth and the shape of the lips. In late Old English, there appear to have been three short vowels pronounced with part of the tongue raised towards the roof of the mouth near the front of the mouth (/æ/, /e/, /i/) and three corresponding long vowels (/æ:/, /e:/, /i:/). These we term **front vowels**. Likewise, there seem to have been three short and three long **back vowel phonemes**, in which the raised part of the tongue is further back in the mouth: /a(:)/, /o(:)/ and /u(:)/. The vowels are also distinguished from one another by the height of the raised part of the tongue in the mouth: in the case of Old English, /a(:)/ and /æ(:)/ are the **low** vowels, /o(:)/ and /e(:)/ are the **mid** vowels, and /u(:)/ and /i(:)/ are the **high** vowels. Thus we can talk about a **high front vowel** such as /i/ or a **mid back vowel** such as /o/, and so on.

The shape of the lips also affects vowel sounds. The sounds /o(:)/ and /u(:)/ are **rounded** sounds: that is, they are pronounced with the lips in a more or less circular shape. The other Old English **phonemes** given above are **unrounded** sounds. There is evidence that early Old English (and some later varieties of Old English) also had **rounded mid** and **high front vowel phonemes** in addition to the **unrounded** ones: these can be represented as /ø(:)/ (mid) and /y(:)/ (high).

There is another kind of vowel **phoneme** we have not yet considered, the **diphthong**. If you try saying the word *mouse* slowly, you will find that the vowel sound is not produced with a single tongue position and a single lip configuration (unless you speak one of the varieties of English in which this **phoneme** is not a **diphthong**: conservative speakers of Scots, for instance, may pronounce the vowel more like /u/, while younger speakers from southeastern England may tend towards /a:/). Instead the sound begins with a **low, unrounded front vowel** and glides to a **high, rounded back vowel**. You should be able to feel your tongue and lips moving, and hear the sound changing as they do. In late Old English there were two such diphthongs, /æa/ and /eo/ (usually spelt <ea> and <eo> respectively), and most scholars believe that there were both long (/æ:a/, /e:o/) and short (/æa/, /eo/) forms of these diphthongs, which were distinct phonemes. Earlier forms of the language also appear to have had long and short /i(:)o/, which usually appears to have lowered its first element and become /e(:)o/, and long and short /i(:)e/, which generally seems to have monophthongised in late Old English, with the result that it is often represented in spelling by <i> or <y>.

Phonemes are the small-scale building blocks of words. However, there are also slightly larger-scale building blocks. The language of the

Anglo-Saxons, Old English (in common with other Germanic languages) was an inflected language. The **inflexions** of a language are the ways in which individual words alter in order to adjust their meanings: in Modern English, for instance, nouns typically have two inflexions, one for the singular (*house*) and one for the plural (*houses*). In Modern English, in other words, the plural **inflexion** is usually the **ending** /z/ or /ɪz/, which is added to the end of the **stem** of the word (so the **stem** is *house* and the **ending** is -*s*, in terms of the standard Modern English spellings). The singular **inflexion** involves no ending (this is known as **zero-inflexion**). Modern English also has an **inflexion** for indicating possession, usually also /z/ or /ɪz/ (but represented in writing by the sequence <'s> in the singular, as in *dog's*, and <s'> in the plural, as in *dogs'*). **Inflexions** need not necessarily be **endings**: in Modern English, for instance, we also have a few nouns that form their plurals by changing the vowel sound in their stem (their **stem vowel**), as in *man* and *men* or *goose* and *geese*. Old English has more inflexions than this, but they are not essential to our purposes here: a good introduction to Old English, including the major features of its inflexional system is Baker (2007); full details of the inflexional system of Old English can be found in Campbell (1959: § 568-768).

It is also possible to form new words by combining words. Thus we can have words like *penknife*, formed by combining the word *pen* with the word *knife*. Such words are known as **compound** words, and the process by which they are produced can be termed **compounding**. In Old English, **compounding** was a very productive source of new **lexis**. However, new words can also be formed by the addition of a **prefix** or **suffix** to a pre-existing word. For instance, the verb *lodge* produces *dislodge* by the addition of the **prefix** *dis-*, while *tickle* produces *ticklish* with the suffix -*ish*. These processes can be termed **affixation**, and they are distinguished from **compounding** by the fact that **prefixes** and **suffixes** are not meaningful on their own.

You should now have a basic model of how words are put together. In the spoken language, each word consists of a sequence of **phonemes**. In Old English (and other early Germanic languages) each **phoneme** is represented in the written language by a **graph**, or sometimes a sequence of **graphs** (usually a sequence of two graphs, a **digraph**). The following diagram is a reminder of the Old English vowel **phonemes** discussed

22

above, together with the **graphs** that late Anglo-Saxon scribes usually used to represent them (note that Anglo-Saxon texts do not normally indicate vowel length in any way):

	Front vowels	Back vowels
High	/i(:)/ <i>, /y(:)/ <y>	/u(:)/ <u>
Mid	/e(:)/ <e>	/o(:)/ <o>
Low	/æ(:)/ <æ>	/ɑ(:)/ <a>
Diphthongs: /æ(:)ɑ/ <ea>, /e(:)o/ <eo>,		/i(:)e/ <ie>

In what follows, whole words in Old English will usually, as is conventional, be given in italics with macrons (horizontal bars placed above vowel symbols) to indicate long vowels: for instance *stān* 'stone'. When individual phonemes or sequences of phonemes are being discussed, however, the notation given in the table above will be employed.

Above the level of the phoneme, we have seen that words can consist of **stems**, which can be altered, usually by the addition of inflexional **endings** (though, as we have seen, other types of **inflexion** are possible), to adjust their meanings (for instance when talking about plural items as opposed to a singular item). New words can be created by the **compounding** of pre-existing words, or by **affixation**.

The life stories of words

The creation of new words by **compounding** and **affixation** brings us on to the broader issue of how languages develop, and the ways in which this impacts on their **lexis**. **Compounding** and **affixation** are, of course, ways in which the existing **lexis** of a language can be used to create new **lexis**. But of course speakers of a language can also make use of the resources of other languages with which they come into contact. Thus speakers of Old English in the north of England came into close and prolonged contact with speakers of Old Norse who settled in this area during the late Anglo-Saxon period, and they borrowed words such as *law* and *fellow* from Old Norse (Campbell 1959: § 566). We call such borrowed words **loanwords**. There is also a process known as **loan-translation**, in which a language uses its own existing **lexis** to create a new term by translating a word or phrase from another language. An example of this is the word

Sunday, which literally translates Latin *solis dies* ('sun's day'). The words employed (*sun* and *day*) are native English words, but they do not simply form a new, native compound, because they are an English translation of the Latin name, and therefore dependent on the Latin name.

We can therefore think of the **lexis** of a language as a huge collection of words to which words can be added by various processes (such as **compounding, affixation,** borrowing and **loan-translation**). Words can be added at different times, according to the needs of speakers to express new ideas, and according to various external factors, such as contact with speakers of other languages. Words can also be lost, either because new words replace them (and there can be various reasons for this), or because they refer to things or concepts that no longer exist: Old English, for instance, possessed the word *þyrs* for some sort of ogre, but apart from the term *thrush* or *hobthrush* in a few areas (*MED*: under *thurs(e)*; Spence 1979: 90-1), this word has more or less died out of English, perhaps because of a loss of belief in the precise sort of ogre termed a *þyrs*, or perhaps because other words, such as *ogre*, have replaced it.

It will also be apparent, however, that words change in pronunciation over time (and this can also occasion changes in spelling). It is particularly important for the arguments in the following chapters that we have a good, basic understanding of the processes involved in this sort of change, which we can term **phonological change** or **sound change.** **Sound changes** can happen for various reasons, and we can sometimes work out the effects of the change without being able to discover the precise reasons for the change. However, one **sound change** whose causes are not totally opaque will serve as a useful example of what we mean by this term. The change in question is known as **i-mutation** (or **i-umlaut**). This change explains noun inflexions such as *man ~ men* and *goose ~ geese*, mentioned above. It also explains the different vowel sounds in related pairs of words like *broad ~ breadth* and *long ~ length*.

The sound change known as **i-mutation** occurred in very early Old English (before we have any substantial written records of the language). The change affected **back vowels** when the vowel of the following syllable was /i/, and the **low** and **mid short front vowels**, also when the vowel of the following syllable was /i/. The change involved the sort of process known as **vowel harmony**, whereby a vowel moves towards the vowel of the following syllable: the tongue and lips begin to move towards the

24

position for the second vowel early, and thus the first vowel is sounded as a vowel closer to the second vowel. In the case of **i-mutation**, this means that **back vowels** are **fronted**, so that they are sounded at the front of the mouth. Thus Old English *gōs* /goːs/ originally had a plural **inflexional ending** containing the sound /i/, which caused /oː/ to be pronounced further forward in the mouth (since /i/ is a **front vowel**) as /øː/ (a sound similar to /eː/ but pronounced with rounded lips). In early texts and in some dialects of late Old English, the mutated plural form is spelt <goes> (representing /gøːs/), using <o> to indicate the **rounded** quality of the vowel, and <e> to indicate that it is a **front vowel**. However, in the West Saxon dialect, the spelling is <ges>, which seems to show that the sound /øː/ produced by **i-mutation** had **unrounded** to match the existing **phoneme** /eː/. The explanation for *broad ~ breadth* and *long ~ length* involves a similar process of **i-mutation**, but in this case the /i/ was part of a derivational **suffix** by which nouns were created from adjectives, rather than forming part of an **inflexional ending** (for details see Campbell 1959: § 589.6).

The examples discussed so far demonstrate that **i-mutation** involved **fronting** of **back vowels**. In fact the full pattern of **i-mutation** of **back vowels** can be summarised as follows:

/u(ː)/ <u> -> /y(ː)/ <y>
/o(ː)/ <o> -> /ø(ː)/ <oe> (unrounded -> /e(ː)/ <e>)
/ɑ(ː)/ <a> -> /æ(ː)/ <æ> (and -> /e(ː)/ <e> before /n/, /m/ and /ŋ/, as in OE *mann ~ menn*)

However, **i-mutation** also affected **low** and **mid short front vowels**: /e/ <e> -> /i/ <i> and /æ/ <æ> -> /e/ <e>. **Diphthongs** could also be subject to **i-mutation**: /ie/ was the result of **i-mutation** of the other Old English diphthongs.

The example of **i-mutation** shows how sounds can affect one another, and cause changes of sounds when certain conditions are met. In the case of **i-mutation**, the necessary condition is the presence of the sound /i(ː)/ (or /j/) in the following syllable (although this sound had generally disappeared by the time that texts began to be written down in Old English). We call such changes **conditioned sound changes**, because a nearby sound provides the necessary conditions for the change to take place. But one can also have **unconditioned sound changes**, changes in which all instances of a particular phoneme change, regardless of the surrounding sounds. An example of an **unconditioned change** that we will come across in a subsequent chapter is the one known as **Second Fronting**. The effects of this change can only be seen in some texts in the Mercian dialect of Old English, which suggests that the change occurred only in a relatively restricted area. However, in this area, the **phoneme** /æ/ <æ> was **raised** to /e/ <e> and /ɑ/ <a> was **fronted** to /æ/ <æ>, producing *feder* 'father' where other dialects have *fæder* and *dægas* 'days' where other dialects have *dagas*. This change affected more or less all instances of /æ/ and /e/ in stressed syllables, regardless of what sounds came before and after them (for details see Campbell 1959: §§ 164-9). It therefore seems that this change occurred whatever the surrounding sounds, and it can thus be termed an **unconditioned change**.

The life stories of languages

We are now ready to consider the ways in which languages develop over long time periods, and how those processes of change are reflected in the lexis of interrelated languages. A language, of course, does not exist independently of the people who speak it, whom we can term the **speech community** (but note that a **speech community** need not be a political or social community). The language continues to exist by virtue of the fact that people continue to use it. This has important implications for how languages develop over time.

If we imagine a very small speech community, where all the members communicate with one another regularly, we would expect that, as **sound changes** affect the speech of individuals within the community, they could quickly spread to the rest of the community. Similarly, we might expect that new words – whether produced by **compounding, affixation,** borrowing or **loan-translation** – could quickly spread across the entire community, and loss of words might also tend to be generalised across the community.

Now if this **speech community** were split in two, say by emigration, we would have two **speech communities** speaking the same language. But this situation would not last indefinitely: each community's language would undergo changes, but, since they would no longer be in close and regular contact, they would not pass on the changes to one another, and their languages would gradually diverge as each community's language underwent a different set of changes. The two speech communities would go through a process by which they slowly moved from the position of speaking two varieties of the same language, to speaking two clearly distinct languages. But these two languages would still be related to one another.

This, in very simple terms, is what has happened to most of the European languages: they have undergone a gradual development from a common ancestor known as Proto-Indo-European. Our main focus is the Germanic languages, which appear to have had a common ancestor (which we can term **Proto-Germanic**) that was itself just one of several descendants of Proto-Indo-European. We can draw a (partial) family tree of the Germanic languages, showing how they descend from **Proto-Germanic**, which looks like this:

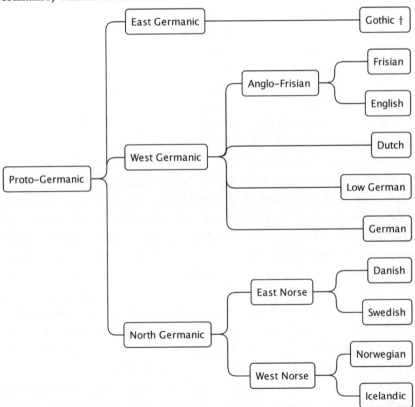

Figure 1. The Germanic languages.

But how do we know that this tree accurately represents the development of the Germanic languages? There are two answers to this question. The first is, it does not – but we will come back to that in a little while. This tree is, of course, a simplification of a very complex set of language situations and developments over many centuries. **Proto-Germanic** (like any language labelled 'Proto-') is not a real language that we have written records of: it is a reconstruction, based on its descendants, for which we do have direct evidence. That does not, however, mean that it is pure invention. The methods involved in reconstructing language family trees are complex, but a brief example should help to demonstrate that there is a robust and principled method of reconstruction that we can employ.

Consider the following list of German and English words:

1	Zeit	tide
2	Zahn	tooth
3	Zahl	tale
4	Zunge	tongue
5	Ziegel	tile
6	treten	tread
7	Trog	trough
8	Zentrum	centre

These words all have closely related meanings. More than that, they also show regular correspondences between their sounds. For example, each of the first five German words begins with /ts/ <z>, while each of the corresponding English words begins with /t/ <t>. Looking at larger samples of German and English words, we would find that such correspondences are common, and that /ts/ at the beginning of a German word is regularly matched by /t/ at the beginning of a word of similar form and meaning in English. We could explain this as the result of pure chance, but a more plausible explanation is that English and German are related, and that a sound change happened in the ancestor of English or German by which either /t/ became /ts/ or /ts/ became /t/. But how might we tell which direction the change went in?

The sixth and seventh word pairs give us a clue as to the direction of the change. The correspondence of German /ts/ at the beginning of a word with English /t/ at the beginning does not hold good for words beginning /tr/ (note that in many varieties of English this sequence is better represented as /tɹ/, and in many German varieties /tʁ/ would be a better representation). In other words, we have evidence here for a conditioned sound change: /t/ followed by /r/ does not undergo any change, appearing with more or less the same sound in German and English. This suggests that /t/ becomes /ts/ in the ancestor of German when followed by a vowel. This would be one conditioned change. On the other hand, two changes would be required if /ts/ was the original form: /ts/ before /r/ would have to become /tr/ in the common ancestor of both English and German, while /ts/ before a vowel would only become /t/ in the ancestor of English. The simplest explanation of the data is, therefore, that /t/ becomes /ts/ before vowels in the ancestor of German. The possibilities are graphically represented in Figure 2.

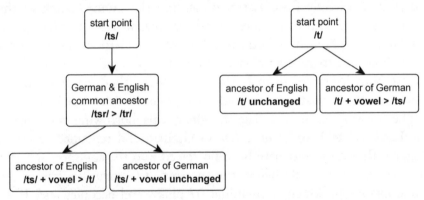

Figure 2. A Germanic sound change: two possible patterns of development.

As the diagram clearly shows, the pattern we have observed in the modern languages can most simply be explained by a starting point of */t/ in the common ancestor of the two languages, rather than */ts/ (asterisks are conventionally used to indicate linguistic forms that are not directly attested in the written records of a language, but can be reconstructed using the sorts of method under discussion here). Careful comparison of many instances of words such as these, words shared by two or more languages through their common ancestor (they are termed **cognate** words), can help to elucidate the **sound changes** by which the languages diverged from one another. At the same time, if we wish to argue that a given set of words are **cognates**, one test we must satisfy is the test of regular sound correspondences: if we have an English word beginning /t/ plus vowel, then we should expect its German cognate to begin /ts/ plus vowel.

The last word listed (*Zentrum - centre*) is the odd one out: it has /ts/ followed by a vowel in German, and so, if the corresponding English word is a cognate, we should expect it to begin with /t/. Instead it begins with /s/. This failure to match the regular sound correspondence alerts us to the fact that *Zentrum* and *centre* are not cognates, although they do look and sound similar, and they do have much the same meaning. The failure of the regular sound correspondence does not, however, mean that they are unrelated: they both derive ultimately from Latin *centrum*, although the English word probably derives from the French descendant of the Latin word, whereas the spelling of the German word suggests a derivation directly from Latin, preserving the <um> ending of the Latin word. In both cases, these words are **loanwords**: they have been borrowed from French or Latin into English and German. They are not alone, however: there is another Latin loanword in our list – *Ziegel* and *tile* are both borrowed from Latin *tegula*. Why, then, do these words follow the regular pattern of sound correspondences discussed above?

The answer lies in the date at which this borrowing took place. For Latin /t/ to have become /ts/ in German and remained as /t/ in English, the word must have been borrowed into the common ancestor of German and English, before the ancestor of German underwent the sound change by which word-initial /t/ plus vowel becomes /ts/. If we look at words beginning with /t/ which were borrowed into German after the period during which this sound change was operative, we would expect them to begin with /t/ rather than /ts/, because they would not be affected by the change. Thus German *Tennis* begins with /t/ rather than /ts/. Words borrowed before the change, or while it was still operative, will begin with /ts/, and this is what we see with *Ziegel*. This sort of evidence can, therefore, be invaluable in building up a picture of when certain words were borrowed into the Germanic languages, and, as D.H. Green (2000: 201-70) has shown, careful scrutiny of what sorts of words were borrowed very early on from Latin into the Germanic languages can provide valuable clues to the nature of early Germanic society and its interactions with the Latin-speaking world.

We can see, then, that careful analysis of the patterns of sounds in

cognate words can help us to build up a picture of what **sound changes** have affected related languages, and from this we can work backwards towards the proto-language. By establishing where languages share **sound changes** we can also begin to determine how closely or distantly related two languages are, and by cross referencing such comparisons against all the other languages in the family, we can move towards drawing the tree we saw above. But we should bear in mind the other answer to the question 'how do we know that this tree accurately represents the development of the Germanic languages?'. Looking at the overall pattern of interrelationships between these languages, the tree is a useful visualisation tool, but it presents a picture that is in some ways misleadingly simple.

If we revisit the basic model of a **speech community** we considered above, we can spot some obvious difficulties. We considered what happens when a **speech community** splits into two with very little communication between the two new communities, but we did not allow for the complexities of human migration, community-forming and so on. We also based our thinking on a very small, homogenous community in which changes were readily spread throughout the community. But if we consider, say, all the people who speak English in the world today as the English speech community, it will readily be apparent that changes are not easily and quickly spread throughout the speech community. Even if we restrict ourselves to British English, it seems clear that there is a lot of variety within the speech community. Changes to the language may well begin in one part of the community (defined by geography, socio-economic class, gender, age, ethnicity and so on) and gradually spread to other parts of it. And a change may not reach all parts of the community. It may be that the use of *wicked* to mean 'good' has spread across the whole geographical area of the British Isles, but we should not hold our breath waiting for this change to enter the speech of elderly professors.

We should also be aware that **sound changes** can have similar limitations: a modern sound change that has been attracting a lot of attention is the development of the /t/ phoneme in English to a glottal stop in **medial** and **final** position in words such as *butter* and *cut*. This change seems originally to have been a feature of southeastern varieties of English, but increasingly it has spread across other parts of the country, especially in the speech of younger people. Perhaps it will eventually be generalised across almost all varieties of British English, but we have not reached that point yet. We can think of the speech community as a little bit like a pond, with changes starting at individual points within the pond, and then rippling across the pond, sometimes reaching all areas of the pond, but sometimes only covering part of it. This model is sometimes known as the **wave model** of language development, and contrasted with the **tree model**, but of course the truth is that both are simplifications of the complexities of linguistic behaviour, and both capture some important ideas about language development. Recent work on the classification of language families has made use of techniques originally developed for working with genetic data to draw network diagrams, which capture aspects of the tree-like quality and the wave-like quality of language families. For a more detailed, but nevertheless very accessible, discussion of the problems and methods of language classification, including recent developments in using genetic models, see McMahon and McMahon (2005).

Names in the Germanic languages

The discussion above should have given you a reasonable idea of how historical linguists reconstruct the interrelationships between languages, and you should have a sense of the role played by **cognates** and **sound changes** in this broader model. These ideas are important background for what follows. However, in what follows we will be focussing in particular on names – the names of deities, of people, and of places. Names behave to some extent in the same ways as ordinary words, but not entirely so.

Early Germanic personal names are generally related to ordinary, meaningful words, and come in two basic flavours: **monothematic** and **dithematic**. A **dithematic** name is formed by combining two words, rather as a **compound** word is formed by the combination of two words. Thus we get Old English **dithematic** names like *Ælfræd* (*ælf* 'elf' + *ræd* 'advice') and *Æþelstān* (*æþel* 'noble' + *stān* 'stone'). In these examples, *ælf* and *æþel* are the **protothemes** (first elements) of the names, and *ræd* and *stān* are the **deuterothemes** (second elements). A **monothematic** name, not surprisingly, is formed from a single root, such as *Wulf* ('wolf') or *Bēda* ('battle'). Such names can also be formed by shortening of

dithematic names, as in the case reported by Bede (in book 2, chapter 5 of his *Ecclesiastical History*) of King Sæbeorht (Bede's spelling seems to have been <saberct>) of the East Saxons, whose sons called him <saba> (see van Els 1972: 166-7; Plummer 1896: 1.91; Colgrave and Mynors 1969: 152-3). In this instance, the **dithematic** name is composed of the words *sæ* 'sea' and *beorht* 'bright', but the **monothematic** derivative *Saba* does not respect the boundary between the two elements of the name. If we did not know that *Saba* was a shortened form of *Sæbeorht*, we might be puzzled by the lack of an ordinary word from which the name could derive – and it may be that quite a few **monothematic** names of obscure origin actually derive from such shortenings. There is also some use of **affixation** in producing Germanic names, typically involving a single root plus a suffix. An example we will return to in a later chapter is *Hreðel*, the name of a Geatish king in *Beowulf*, whose name consists of the single root *hreð* plus a diminutive suffix that also appears in personal names in other Germanic languages, for instance in the name *Wulfila* ('little wolf') borne by the ecclesiastic credited with translating parts of the bible into Gothic (Marchand 1973: 13).

There was a limited stock of ordinary words that could be employed as name elements: it was not a free for all on the entire lexis of the language. And a name element derived from an ordinary word did not necessarily develop in the same way as that word: the word might undergo **sound changes**, or fall out of use, and the name element could remain unchanged. Equally, a name element might undergo a **sound change** that the word did not, as a result of being combined with another element. Name elements can, therefore, preserve archaic forms of words, or even archaic words. This means that Germanic language speakers did not necessarily always see their names as related to meaningful words (as the example of *Saba* suggests), but in some cases they clearly did make the connection, as in the case of Æthelred the Unready. His nickname – which is first attested in the thirteenth century in the form *unrad*, and is better translated 'of bad advice' than 'unready' – plays on the **deuterotheme** *ræd* 'advice' of his name, which, together with the **prototheme** *æþel* 'noble', could be taken to suggest that Æthelred was an individual blessed with 'noble advice' (Lapidge et al. 2001: under *Æthelred the Unready*).

The situation with place-names is not unlike that with personal names, but there is a very important difference: place-names were coined to describe the place being named, whereas personal names were not coined to describe the child being named. It is possible that calling one's son *Æþelstān* expresses a general wish that they will grow up to be noble and strong, but a babe in arms can hardly be literally – or even metaphorically – described as a 'noble stone'. Germanic place-names, however, seem generally to have been descriptions of the place being named, sometimes with a single word (as in *Harrow*, from Old English *hearg* 'site of pagan worship') and sometimes with two words (as in *Charlton*, from Old English *ceorla tūn* 'peasants' farm'). Place-names with more elements are also possible, but rarer, and **affixation** can also occur, as in the place-name *Reading* (Old English *Rēadingas* 'followers of Rēada', formed of the personal name *Rēada* with the suffix *-ing* 'descendant, follower'). In this case the name describes the place by indicating who lives there. Once a place-name has formed, it can continue in use for many centuries, and the original meaning can be obscured by **sound changes** or by loss from the language of the word or words from which the name was originally formed. Thus *Surrey* derives from Old English *sūðer* 'southern' plus **gē* 'district', but even by the period in which most records of Old English were written down, the word **gē* had fallen out of use, and although *sūðer* is (indirectly) related to Modern English *southern*, changes in pronunciation (and spelling) of the name *Surrey* have obscured the link. It is therefore crucially important, in attempting to determine the origins of place-names, to find the earliest records of the name, which are likely to record it in a form that more readily reveals the word or words from which it was originally formed. Nevertheless, even with early records, not all place-names are readily decipherable.

Electronic corpora

The characteristics of languages discussed above can only be determined by assembling evidence of the languages themselves. In the case of languages spoken today, one can collect data directly from speakers of the languages under study, but of course this is not the case in working with medieval languages. The data for these languages exist only in written form, and assembling large bodies of such data from manuscripts, or even from modern printed editions of manuscripts, is a time-consuming undertaking. Data from such sources features throughout this book, but electronic corpora are also employed, and a brief word about these may prove useful to those who are unfamiliar with them.

The *Dictionary of Old English Corpus* (*DOEC*) is a database containing a copy of almost every extant text in Old English. This means that the database gives a good picture of the Old English language as a whole, as far as we are able to gather data on it. However, it does have its limitations. The database does not usually record the different versions of a text in all the extant manuscripts: texts in the database are often taken from printed editions, and therefore simply represent the edited text, ignoring manuscript variants. Cross-checking material in the corpus against the printed editions, and sometimes against the manuscript or manuscripts of a text, can be important in order to verify specific readings. In what follows, *DOEC* is used to check for overall patterns in the Old English language, where the large number of texts in the corpus allows us to draw reasonably safe conclusions about the language as a whole. Every text within *DOEC* has a unique identifying number known as a Cameron number (the preparatory list of texts that was compiled for the project is Cameron 1973), and searches can be restricted to individual Cameron numbers or groups of Cameron numbers. This enables us to look for patterning within specific texts or groups of texts, and this technique has also been employed.

One area where *DOEC* is not always helpful, however, is in dealing with names. While *DOEC* has attempted to collect all texts in which Old English is employed, even as individual words (as in a Latin-Old English glossary), it does not include texts in other languages in which Old English personal names or place-names appear. In what follows, Old English personal names recorded in Latin texts are particularly important. Fortunately, a resource has become available in recent years that provides much better coverage of such names. This is the *Prosopography of Anglo-Saxon England* (*PASE*). *PASE* is intended to provide information about the inhabitants of Anglo-Saxon England, and it therefore attempts to identify individuals and collect together basic information about them, including their status, occupations, possessions, and places and people they were involved with. Each individual is, of necessity, listed under one form of their name (usually, but not always, a form that appears in medieval sources), but the database also collects the recorded forms of their names in the various sources that mention them. The recorded name forms can be used as a corpus by the linguist interested in Old English personal names, with a search function that allows wildcard searching. Work on *PASE* is ongoing, with some sources still to be added (for instance, at the time of writing the names of kings and moneyers on Anglo-Saxon coins seem to be largely if not wholly absent from this database). Nevertheless, it already provides a usefully large sample of Old English personal names, and is used below in identifying elements employed in forming such names.

3

The Romano-Germanic Religious
Landscape and the Early Middle Ages

There are a large number of votive inscriptions of the late Roman period
in which Germanic, Romano-Germanic and Celto-Germanic deities are
named. Derks' study of votive inscriptions of the lower Rhine area gives a
total of 1112 inscriptions, with 655 instances of what Derks terms 'native
name[s]' (that is, Germanic and Celtic names), 42 instances of 'double
name[s]' (names 'consisting of a Roman and a native component') and 415
instances of 'Roman name[s]' (1998: 92-3). In this corpus of inscriptions,
there is a considerable variety of different deities, some of whom appear
as individuals, a few as paired goddesses, and many as groups of goddesses
with collective names or epithets. There is a fairly lengthy history of
research into these inscriptions and the deities named on them, and only
a brief survey of this material will be possible here, focussing on the major
areas of debate and the main outlines of what is known about these deities.
As we shall see, much of the recent work on them has been focussed on
understanding their cults within their late Roman contexts, and considering
them as social and political phenomena conditioned by interactions between
Romans and native societies in northwest Europe.

However, the development of research on such deities has also been
marked by a number of attempts to integrate them into accounts of
Germanic pre-Christian religious life. These will be discussed separately,
as the methodologies employed in such work, and the conclusions
reached, are central to the aims of this book, which seeks to suggest
some new ways of approaching the relationships between late Roman
and early medieval evidence for pre-Christian cults. We must turn first
to the votive inscriptions themselves, and what they can tell us about
pagan deities with Germanic or partially Germanic names in the late

Roman period. It will be convenient to consider these under two broad categories: gods and goddesses on the one hand, and matrons on the other (Mees 2006: 14 expresses misgivings about the use of the term 'matron', but I retain it here as it has become the normal term for these deities among modern scholars). As will become apparent, however, the distinction between goddesses and matrons is far from clear-cut.

Gods and goddesses

There are relatively few gods with Germanic or partially Germanic names in Roman-period votive inscriptions. Derks' study, which, as noted above, does not distinguish between Celtic and Germanic names, notes only 10 instances of inscriptions to gods with a native name, and 42 to those with a double name – the name of a Roman god and a Germanic name or epithet (1998: 92). The three Roman deities whose names most commonly appear in such inscriptions around the Rhine Frontier area are Hercules, Mars and Mercury. The name *Hercules* is usually paired with forms of the term *Magusanus*: votive inscriptions to Hercules Magusanus (here and throughout I follow the convention of giving names of Romano-Germanic deities in the nominative form, although they usually appear only in oblique forms in inscriptions) are mainly distributed around the northern end of the Rhine, suggesting a connection between this deity and the Batavi (Derks 1991: 249-51; Derks 1998: 98-9). The names *Mars* and *Mercury*, on the other hand, appear with a range of epithets or names, although few can certainly be identified as linguistically Germanic rather than Celtic. Two whose names seem to link them clearly with Germanic groups are Mars Thingsus and Mercurius Cimbrianus. The term *Thingsus*, which appears in an inscription set up by Frisian soldiers serving in the Roman garrison at Housteads on Hadrian's Wall, is generally taken to relate to the ancestor of Old Norse *þing* 'legal assembly' and Old English *þing*, which can also have the senses 'assembly/court of law/legal case' (Green 2000: 34). This might indicate a deity with a particular function in legal contexts, or perhaps more broadly a deity associated with a social grouping through its assembly. *Cimbrianus* appears to be a more straightforwardly tribal epithet, indicating a relationship between the deity and the tribe known as the *Cimbri* (Simek 1993: 212-13).

3. The Romano-Germanic Religious Landscape and the Early Middle Ages

There are relatively few deities recorded on Roman-period inscriptions who are termed *dea* ('goddess') and have names or epithets that appear to derive from a Germanic language. Part of the difficulty in identifying such goddesses lies in the problems of establishing whether a name is Celtic or Germanic. There are also some deities (including some paired deities) whose names are recorded without a generic term such as *dea* that might guide our interpretation of them. The paired deities include the Alaisiagis, who appear alongside Mars Thingsus (discussed above) in three votive inscriptions, and the Ahuecannae. The Alaisiagis are recorded once with the individual names *Baudihillie* and *Friagabi*, once with the names *Bede* and *Fimmilene*, and once without individual names (Birley 1986: 77; Stolte 1986: 655-6). The Ahuecannae appear on one votive inscription, with the individual names *Aveha* and *Hellivesa* (Stolte 1986: 650).

Among the probably Germanic individual goddesses we can place Hariasa and Harimella, whose names both appear to be formed with a derivative of Proto-Germanic **harja-* 'army' (Old English *here*), and Hludana, whose name can be related to the English word *loud* (Old English *hlud*) and its cognates in other Germanic languages (Stolte 1986: 652, 659-60). Given the difficulties of determining the linguistic make-up of such names, a thorough new study based on systematic analysis of epigraphic practice and the recording of Germanic personal names in Roman-period Latin texts is very much in order, but it is not the purpose of this volume to provide such a study (Mees 2006 provides a useful linguistic survey of the epigraphic material from the Rhineland, but more remains to be done).

There is, however, one point about the linguistic properties of these names that we should particularly bear in mind: there are a number of points of overlap between the words used in forming the names mentioned above and the words that formed part of the Germanic stock of personal name elements. Thus **harja-* appears as an element in personal names in various Germanic languages, such as *Charibert*, *Charigisil*, *Chlothachari* and *Harigast* (Reichert 1987-90: under *Charibert*, *Charigisil*, *Chlothachari*, *Harigast*; see also 2.535-9). The first element of *Baudihillie* is probably a Germanic word meaning 'battle' (from which Old English *beadu* 'battle' derives), and this word also appears as a name element across a variety of Germanic languages, as in *Baudegisil*,

Baudimund, *Hariobaud* and *Merobaud* (Reichert 1987-90: under *Baudegisil*, *Baudimund*, *Hariobaud*, *Merobaud*; see also 2.477-9). This element also probably appears in the name *Baduhenna* – apparently the name of a goddess – mentioned by Tacitus in his *Annals* (Fisher 1906: book 4, chapter 73). The name *Friagabi* is clearly dithematic, and both elements can be seen as related to elements used in forming personal names: *fria* can be related to the element that Reichert (1987-90: 2.508) records as *frī-* in names such as *Frianni*, *Friard*, *Friobaud* and *Friomath*; *gabi* is connected with the element that appears in Old English as *giefu* 'gift', in names such as *Æþelgiefu*, resulting in interpretations of *Friagabi* as meaning 'friendly giving' (Simek 1993: under *Friagabis*) or 'die liebe Geberin' ('the dear giver'; Gutenbrunner 1936: 90). The name of the goddess Vagdavercustis – who was probably worshipped among the Batavi or Cugerni (Stolte 1986: 652-3) – is perhaps related to a male personal name *Vagdavercustus*. Although I do not share Birley's certainty that the latter name is 'manifestly Germanic' and applied to 'a son of votaries of Vagdavercustis' (Birley 1986: 76), the association of the goddess with the Batavi or Cugerni would at least be consistent with an interpretation of her as Germanic.

This raises questions about whether the names of these goddesses should be interpreted in terms of roles or functions performed by them – as, for instance, Stolte implicitly does in classing Hariasa and Harimella as 'Kriegsgöttinnen' ('war-goddesses') on the basis of the use of the element **harja-* in their names (1986: 652). It is possible that role or function determined these name patterns, and that human personal names were influenced by patterns of sacral naming – but we should not discount the possibility that sacral naming could be patterned in part on human naming. In the case of the matrons, as we shall see, there is clear evidence for development of matron names from the names of human socio-political groupings, and it may be that goddesses could develop in similar ways. The possibility of similar patterns of development in goddesses and matrons should not surprise us, given that they do not always seem to have formed distinct categories. There are cases where goddesses appear in plural form, possibly as the result of connections with the cult patterns evident among the matrons (Stolte 1986: 620-1; Rüger 1987: 3). There are also instances of the deities usually referred to as the *matronae Aufaniae* (discussed below) appearing in inscriptions as *deae Aufaniae* (Gutenbrunner 1936: 208-9). To attempt to draw an absolute distinction between goddesses and matrons, therefore, seems inconsistent with the available evidence.

Matrons

The matrons (referred to by the Latin terms *matronae, matres* or **matrae*) are by far the most common type of deity in the votive inscriptions. Over a thousand individual inscriptions attest to matrons (Kolbe 1960: 118), and Neumann (1987) discusses 56 different names in his article on Germanic matron-names. A rather larger number are included in the handlist of such names compiled by Gutenbrunner (1936), although many of these are marked as doubtful by Gutenbrunner, either because their attestation is dubious, or because it is not certain that they are Germanic. Gutenbrunner's handlist clearly requires updating, but unfortunately it seems that a planned new index of these inscriptions by C.B. Rüger and B. Beyer-Rotthoff is now unlikely to be published (Mees 2006: 37). Many of the matron-names are attested only in one or a few inscriptions, but the Austriahenae and the Aufaniae stand out as significant cult figures, with well over a hundred extant inscriptions to the former (Kolbe 1960: 53), while the latter are attested not only around their cult centre of Bonn, but as far afield as Lyon and Carmona (Rüger 1987: 22). The matrons appear to have had a well-established iconography, with many depictions of them on votive stones as three seated female figures, often with bowls of fruit on their laps, though sometimes with other attributes such as bread, money and spinning gear (Garman 2008: 38-9). It is possible, however, that they are also depicted on other artefacts (often as three female figures, but differing in other respects) in contexts without inscriptions that could identify the figures as matrons (Schauerte 1987; Derks 1998: 119). Such anepigraphic depictions are more widely distributed than the votive stones to matrons, which, according to Rüger (1987: 4-9), are clustered in four main geographical concentrations: two to the south, one centred on the Rhone valley, and the other further east, and two to the north, one centred on the Rhine frontier and one on Hadrian's Wall (I omit a smaller cluster Rüger notes in northern Spain). Figure 3 shows the distribution of matrons and goddesses with Germanic names recorded

41

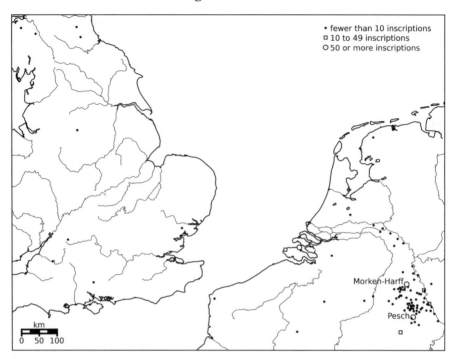

Figure 3. Distribution of Romano-Germanic votive inscriptions to female deities. This map does not incorporate some finds of votive inscriptions since Gutenbrunner (1936), but the overall distribution pattern remains representative. The frequencies are calculated from the number of times each individual matron or goddess appears on separate inscriptions: where more than one deity appears on an inscription, the inscription is therefore represented more than once in the frequency data.

in Gutenbrunner (1936), with the addition of the finds of votive stones to the Austriahenae recorded in Kolbe (1960).

These four concentrations are explicable partly in terms of patterns of military service within the Roman Empire, and partly in terms of distinctive types of matron-cult. The cluster in the Rhone valley consists of matrons with Celtic and Romano-Celtic names or epithets, and this cult appears to have been in existence by the early first century AD (Rüger 1987: 11-13). The cluster to the east of the Rhone valley cluster is composed of matrons without distinguishing names or epithets: here the inscriptions are simply to *matronae*, or sometimes to *iunones* 'Junos' (Rüger 1987: 4). The cluster on the lower Rhine consists of matrons whose names or epithets relate to Germanic and Celtic terms, although they are commonest in the area inhabited by the Ubii (Derks 1998: 119). The cluster on Hadrian's Wall can plausibly be associated with the worship of matrons by soldiers from the lower Rhine area who were serving in Britain (Rüger 1987: 8-9).

The Hadrian's Wall cluster is, therefore, a secondary distribution, which can be seen as an offshoot of the lower Rhine cluster (Rüger 1987: 8). The three main clusters, moreover, can be seen to represent distinct groups of deities: we do not see the same matron-names occurring in all three clusters, and in fact the overall composition of the set of names in use differs markedly between the lower Rhine and the Rhone valley, while the cluster centred on northern Italy is different again in not employing matron-names. Whether or not we should see these three clusters as linked lies outside the scope of this discussion. What is important for our purposes here is that they represent three substantially different cults, whether or not those cults could have had a common origin.

The origins of the lower Rhine matron-cults, however, are worth considering. Recent work has tended to focus on the lower Rhine matrons as native deities undergoing processes of Romanisation. Rüger (1987: 24) suggested that the lower Rhine matrons represented Romanisations of pre-existing native deities of a non-anthropomorphic type. Derks (1998: 124-7) quite rightly rejects this claim, arguing instead that the matrons can be seen as evidence for an ancestor cult that existed prior to the Romanisation of the area. The preponderance of inscriptions in the Ubian area is not, Derks argues, the product of a specifically Ubian origin or focus for the cult, but rather results from the presence of soldiers of north Italian origin in the area around Cologne: these soldiers would have been familiar with the cult of unnamed matrons from north Italy, and could have introduced Roman-style votive inscriptions into the similar native cult on the lower Rhine (Derks 1998: 128).

Derks' argument is an attractive one, and, if correct, it has some important consequences for our understanding of the lower Rhine matron-cults. Gutenbrunner (1936: 117) suggests that the terms *matronae* and *matres* reflected two more or less distinct sub-groups within the matron-cults, with matron-names paired with the term *matres* often deriving from tribal names. According to Derks (1998: 120), however, 'inscriptions in which both terms occur alongside each other and dedications in which the customary form of address *matronae* is replaced by *matres*, make it clear that there was no sharp distinction'. Yet Derks' own argument for the influence of the cult of the unnamed matrons of upper Italy suggests that there is a distinction, although not one which turns around a distinctive use of *matres* for tribal matrons.

The term *matronae* is the preferred term for the unnamed matrons, and it is therefore not surprising that this term should be common in the votive stones of the Ubian area, set up to deities of that specific locality. As Derks points out, such deities as those termed the *matres Hiannanefatae, matres Remae* and *matres Treverae* can best be understood as reflecting the tribal affiliation of those who set up inscriptions to them (1998: 127). The geographical situation of these individuals is of central importance here, in Derks' view: 'staying outside their home *civitas,* these worshippers would not have invoked the ancestors of their strictly local community, but (in the same way as the Lower Rhine soldiers stationed at Hadrian's Wall) the mythical mothers of the larger *civitas* community' (1998: 127). The apparent distinction between tribal *matres* and more locally defined *matronae* is, therefore, probably an accident of cultural interactions in the Ubian area, as Derks argues; but, more than that, the use of the terms *matres* and *matronae* themselves can be attributed to this pattern of development. The term *matronae* can be understood as an import from upper Italy, while the term *matres* appears to reflect a terminology that may have been in more widespread use along the lower Rhine. This usage has been substantially obscured by the fact that the practice of setting up votive stones to matrons centred mainly on the Ubian area, where the term *matronae* had gained currency. The development of an erroneous form **matrae* from *matres* seems to confirm that this form may better reflect less high status conceptions of the matron-cults, while *matronae* perhaps reflects higher status forms of devotion.

This tells us some important things about the nature of the matron-cults. If *matres* was indeed the more widespread (albeit less well-attested) term for the matrons, then this suggests that they were normally understood as mothers, rather than more generally as ladies, as the term *matronae* might suggest (Neumann 1987: 129). Moreover, it is possible that the term *matronae* represents a Gaulish word with the sense 'mother goddess', rather than the Latin word meaning 'lady, married woman' (Mees 2006: 14). This provides some support for the claims for an association between the Anglo-Saxon pre-Christian festival *modranect* ('night of the mothers'), mentioned by Bede, and the matron-cults (Meaney 1985: 5-6; North 1997: 227). The evidence, such as it is, seems to point in the direction of collective deities imagined, at least in part, in terms of kin relationships. This is also supported by some of the naming strategies evidenced by the matron-names.

In his invaluable study of the language of the Germanic matron-names, Neumann identifies four main naming strategies among these names: derivation from place-names, hydronyms (usually river- and stream-names), ethnic terms, and from meaningful words that indicate the activities of the matrons (1987: 109-11). Some examples of names deriving from those of ethnic groups have been noted above, and this group is largely unproblematic. The hydronymic matron-names include names like *Aumenahenae*, *Nersihenae* and *Renahenae*, some of which can be related to particular rivers in the lower Rhine area, while others can be identified linguistically with common hydronymic terms (Neumann 1987: 110). Names deriving from meaningful words require careful argumentation if they are to be supported, as we saw in the case of the *diis hveteris* (see pp. 15-16). The category of matron-names deriving from place-names is also problematic, as we have only very sparse records of place-names in the lower Rhine area in the late Roman period. Neumann discusses a number of difficult cases, and shows that previous identifications with currently attested place-names are not always plausible (1987: 109-10). In a few examples for which Roman period attestations of place-names are available, it is clear that the place-names are in fact derivatives of sub-tribal group-names: for example, the name *matronae Ettrahenae* is evidently related to the *curia Etratium* ('community/district of the Etrates'), a place-name which implies a small-scale socio-political grouping known as the **Etrates* (Derks 1998: 123).

We have evidence, then, for matron-names relating to specific geographical features, particularly rivers, as well as names which relate to local socio-political groupings such as the **Etrates*. Whether these groups should, as Derks argues (1998: 123-4), be considered kin groups in which kinship is to some degree socially constructed, rather than determined purely by family relationships, is a question that lies outside the scope of this book. More importantly, these names appear to contrast with the names that derive from the larger-scale groupings that we normally

45

term tribes, and, as we have seen, Derks has suggested that this reflects different practices of worshippers depending on whether they are setting up an inscription within or outside their own home area (Derks 1998: 127). This suggests, then, that matron-cults were often quite tightly localised, but that to some extent the various different groups worshipping matrons recognised them more generally as a type of deity who operated at tribal and sub-tribal levels: broader or narrower groupings of matrons might therefore be invoked in differing circumstances, thus producing some of the variation in matron-names. So we have variation in names according to the social breadth (or inclusiveness) of the group of matrons whom a worshipper was addressing, and according to tribal and local constructions of worshippers' identities. The deities named the *matres Italis Germanis Gallis Brittis*, to whom an inscription from Winchester attests, also suggest the possibility of supra-tribal grouping of matrons (Gutenbrunner 1936: 215). We can therefore posit an approximate model of the groupings of matrons as shown in Table 1.

dedicators distant from home locality	pan-tribal/wide area name					
	tribal name			tribal name		
dedicators within home locality	local/kin name	local/kin name	local/kin name	local/kin name	local/kin name	local/kin name

Table 1. Matron names and localities.

It must be stressed that this is a simplification of what was no doubt a complex situation, and it attempts only to draw out some common, but not necessarily universal, patterns. In particular, we should note that distance from home locality need not be defined purely in terms of geographical distance. Thus the *matres tramarinae* (or *transmarinae*) appear on a number of inscriptions from Roman Britain set up by members of Germanic units within the Roman army (Collingwood and Wright 1965: nos 919, 920, 1224), as well as in a number of inscriptions where the dedicator's ethnic affiliations are not recorded (Collingwood and Wright 1965: nos 1030, 1224, 1318, 1989). In this case the form of reference for the matrons is determined not simply by the dedicator's distance from home, but by the presence of a sea between the dedicator and their home. The interposition of significant socio-political boundaries may also be a factor: an example of this is furnished by the *matres Germanis Suebis*, evidenced in an inscription from Cologne, whose name indicates connections with a tribal grouping east of the Rhine (Gutenbrunner 1936: 225). The dedicator, who was presumably of Suebian extraction, was perhaps not very distant from home in the Cologne area, but the fact of being within the Empire, while the Suebian homelands were outside it, may have prompted a sense of distance which encourages the use of a tribal term as well as the broader ethnic designation *Germanis* (whether or not this term is a Roman ethnic classification imposed upon Germanic groups is not important in this context: clearly this dedicator recognised the term as relevant in some way to their situation). On the other hand, it is also possible that the dedicator was one of the Suebi Nicretes who were settled within the Empire but at a considerable distance from Cologne (Carroll 2001: 30-1).

Romano-Germanic epigraphy and pre-Christian religious life

There is, then, a large and complex body of evidence for pre-Christian religious life in late Roman epigraphy, which provides an opportunity to study numerous named deities who do not feature among the great gods discussed in Chapter 1. The discussion above is little more than a sketch of some of the broad outlines of the situation, for a longer book would be required to do justice to this body of material. Nevertheless, we have been able to observe some important patterns: the gods and goddesses present a mixed picture of larger, public cults and smaller, perhaps more socially restricted, cults; the matrons, on the other hand, seem generally to reflect local cults, specific to small-scale socio-political groupings, perhaps kin groups (though not necessarily biologically defined). Even if we believe that the great gods were widespread and uniformly important, we must still reckon with the existence of many smaller cults, which should caution us against seeking always to relate evidence for religious life to the cults of the great gods. We have also seen some overlap between goddesses and matrons, which suggests that we should not necessarily expect different cult patterns, although of course some goddesses, such as Nehalennia (Stuart and Bogaers 2001: 44), seem to have enjoyed more public (though not necessarily geographically widespread) cults. There are also clear links between the naming patterns employed for matrons and goddesses and those employed in naming human individuals and groups. As we shall see in the following chapters, these patterns fit well with the evidence for Eostre and Hreda.

4

Eostre: Pan-Germanic Goddess or 'Etymological Fancy'?

In chapter 15 of *De Temporum Ratione* ('On the Reckoning of Time'), Bede discusses the English names of the months. He provides a listing of the English names, together with brief discussions of their etymologies, summarised in Table 2.

Month name	Interpretation	Translation	Latin month
giuli	'a conversione solis in auctum diei'	'from the day when the Sun turns back [and begins] to increase'	January
solmonath	'potest dici mensis placentarum quas in eo diis suis offerebant'	'can be called "month of cakes", which they offered to their gods in that month'	February
hredmonath	'a dea illorum Hreda, cui in illo sacrificabant, nominatur'	'is named for their goddess Hretha, to whom they sacrificed at this time'	March
eosturmonath	'a dea illorum quae Eostre vocabatur et cui in illo festa celebrabant nomen habuit'	'called after a goddess of theirs named Eostre, in whose honour feasts were celebrated in that month'	April
thrimilchi	'dicebatur quod tribus vicibus in eo per diem pecora mulgerentur'	'was so called because in that month the cattle were milked three times a day'	May
lida	'dicitur blandus sive navigabilis quod in	'means "gentle" or "navigable", because in both these months	June
lida	utroque illo mense et blanda sit serenitas aurarum et navigari soleant aequora'	the calm breezes are gentle, and they were wont to sail upon the smooth sea'	July
vveodmonath	'mensis zizaniorum quod ea tunc maxime abundent'	'means "month of tares", for they are very plentiful then'	August
halegmonath	'mensis sacrorum'	'means "month of sacred rites" '	September
vvinterfilleth	'potest dici composito novo nomine hiemiplenium'	'can be called by the invented composite name "winter-full" '	October
blodmonath	'mensis immolationum quod in eo pecora quae occisuri erant diis suis voverent'	' "month of immolations", for then the cattle which were to be slaughtered were consecrated to their gods'	November
giuli	*see above*		December
	(Jones 1943: 212-13)	(Wallis 1999: 54)	

Table 2. Bede's Old English month-names.

Some of Bede's etymologies are evidently correct, such as his interpretation of *vveodmonath* as 'mensis zizaniorum' ('month of weeds'). Others are very problematic, such as *solmonath*: there is no clear evidence for an Old English word **sol* meaning 'cake', and there has therefore been considerable debate as to Bede's exact meaning and the state of his knowledge of pre-Christian offerings (Page 1995: 125-7). Our principal concern here, however, is with the discussion of *hredmonath* (March) and *eosturmonath* (April), as Bede accounts for these two month-names by invoking the names of two pre-Christian goddesses, Hreda and Eostre. We will return to Hreda in the next chapter, but we will begin by discussing Eostre, as somewhat more evidence for her survives, and she has, accordingly, been the subject of rather more modern scholarly attention.

There has been a long history of efforts to discredit Bede's basic claim that there was a pre-Christian goddess called *Eostre*. As early as the late nineteenth century, Weinhold (1869: 52) claimed that 'die angelsächsische Eostre sieht nach einer Erfindung Bedas aus' ('the Anglo-Saxon Eostre looks like an invention by Bede'). Knobloch (1959) suggests that there was no Germanic goddess Eostre, and that in fact the name of the month arises as a loan-translation of the Latin term *albae*. This Latin word is sometimes applied to Easter, but also develops in the later Romance languages into a word for 'dawn' (as in French *aube*). Knobloch (1959: 42-4) argues that the Old English word *ēastre* (and the corresponding Old High German *ôstarun*) was a word denoting the dawn that developed as a translation of the Latin *albae*. As Green (2000: 352-3) points out, however, this is a decidedly tenuous line of argument; and, as we shall see, there is little reason to associate the name *Eostre* or the word *ēastre* with the dawn. More recently, Page (1995: 125) has argued that '*Eostre* is an etymological fancy on Bede's part', and in the most substantial contribution to the debate of recent years – an entire book devoted to the term *Easter* – Udolph (1999) argues that *Easter* developed in a Christian context from a Germanic term for the act of baptism.

These specific attacks on the credibility of Eostre have begun to influence general reference works. The *Dictionary of Old English* has apparently concluded that the debate is settled: 'Bede's derivation of the name from a pre-Christian Anglo-Saxon festival of a goddess *Eastre* is no longer accepted' (*DOE*: under *ēastre*). Another recent reference work,

Roud (2006: 106-7), apparently follows Page's arguments for Bede's invention of Eostre and Hreda. The transmission of this notion into such works of general reference may well give the impression to the wider public that there is no longer any room for debate, and that the case has been decided once and for all against the goddesses. Sermon (2008), however, argues for the existence of Eostre, though his work is marred by poor handling of linguistic evidence. We will consider below some further arguments that will, hopefully, provide reasons for trusting Bede's testimony on the goddess Eostre.

Attempts to cast doubt on Bede's claim for a goddess Eostre have been motivated, in part, by the rather dubious claims which have been made for the character of this goddess, and the extent and nature of her cult. The classic discussion of the goddess Eostre is Jacob Grimm's in his *Deutsche Mythologie*:

> The two goddesses, whom Beda (De temporum ratione cap. 13) cites very briefly, without any description, merely to explain the months named after them, are *Hrede* and *Eástre*, March taking its Saxon name from the first, and April from the second [...]
>
> It would be uncritical to saddle this father of the church, who everywhere keeps heathenism at a distance, and tells us less of it than he knows, with the invention of these goddesses. [...]
>
> We Germans to this day call April *ostermonat*, and *ôstarmânoth* is found as early as Eginhart (temp. Car. Mag.). The great christian festival, which usually falls in April or the end of March, bears in the oldest of OHG. remains the name *ôstarâ* gen. -ûn; it is mostly found in the plural, because two days (ôstartagâ, aostortagâ, Diut. 1, 266ª) were kept at Easter. This *Ostarâ*, like the AS. *Eástre*, must in the heathen religion have denoted a higher being, whose worship was so firmly rooted, that the christian teachers tolerated the name, and applied it to one of their own grandest anniversaries. All the nations bordering on us have retained the Biblical 'pascha'; even Ulphilas writes paska, not áustrô, though he must have known the word; the Norse tongue also has imported its pâskir, Swed. påsk, Dan. paaske. The OHG. adv. *ôstar* expresses movement toward the rising sun (Gramm. 3, 205), likewise the ON. *austr*, and probably an AS. eástor and Goth. áustr. In Latin the identical *auster* has been

pushed round to the noonday quarter, the South. In the Edda a male being, a spirit of light, bears the name of *Austri*, so a female one might have been called *Austra*; the High German and Saxon tribes seem on the contrary to have formed only an *Ostarâ*, *Eástre* (fem.), not Ostaro, Eástra (masc.). And that may be the reason why the Norsemen said pâskir and not austrur: they had never worshipped a goddess Austra, or her cultus was already extinct.

Ostara, *Eástre* seems therefore to have been the divinity of the radiant dawn, of upspringing light, a spectacle that brings joy and blessing, whose meaning could be easily adapted to the resurrection-day of the christian's God. (Grimm 1882-88: 1.289-91)

This has remained an influential statement of the case for Eostre, but it has a number of weaknesses that critics, such as those mentioned above, have pointed out. Most importantly, there is no direct evidence for Grimm's Ostara: she is an extrapolation from the Anglo-Saxon Eostre, and the existence of common terms for Easter in Old English and in southeastern dialects of Old High German. Grimm's interpretation of the role or function of Eostre as a dawn goddess is also problematic; and variations such as Helm's claim that the idea of dawn was here extended to the dawn of the year, when the days lengthened after the spring equinox, and thus to a Spring goddess, do not carry conviction (Helm 1950: 9).

We have, then, a lengthy history of arguments for and against Bede's goddess Eostre, with some scholars taking fairly extreme positions on either side. Much of this debate, however, was necessarily conducted in ignorance of a key piece of evidence, as it was not discovered until 1958. This evidence is furnished by over 150 Romano-Germanic votive inscriptions to deities named the *matronae Austriahenae*, found near Morken-Harff and datable to around 150-250 AD (Kolbe 1960: 53, 122; see Figure 3 on p. 42 for location). Only a few of the votive stones are complete, but many have enough text to be reasonably sure that they were dedicated to the Austriahenae (Kolbe 1960: 55-109). As Gutenbrunner (1966: 123-5) recognised, the first element of the name *Austriahenae* can be connected etymologically with the name *Eostre*, and with an element used in forming Germanic personal names – connections that will be discussed in detail below. Gutenbrunner's proposed interpretation of the evidence, however, relies on a cryptic allusion in an Old Norse eddaic poem to construct a rather unconvincing picture of a Germanic pre-Christian tree festival (1966: 122-3). Sermon (2008: 340), on the other hand, argues that the inscriptions to the Austriahenae 'provide important comparative evidence' for Eostre, but argues that they might be evidence of either the same deity or for deities whose cults 'developed independently'. The possibility of an etymological connection between the names *Eostre* and *Austriahenae* has also led to an argument by Kurt Oertel on a contemporary pagan website that there was indeed a deity Eostre/Austro, connected with the Spring and worshipped across England and parts of the Continent (Oertel 2003). Essentially, Oertel sees the Austriahenae as bolstering the claims of Grimm and Helm, and the implication of his piece is that these matrons are basically figures identical with, or derived from, the goddess Eostre/Austro. This does not seem entirely satisfactory, and in order to unpick the various problems presented by Eostre, we will need to consider not only the exact nature of the deities termed the *matronae Austriahenae*, but also the linguistic evidence provided by Germanic terms for Easter and related words.

'Easter' in the Germanic languages

We turn first to the problem of Germanic terms for Easter. As noted above, Grimm conjectures a goddess named *Ostara*, cognate with the Anglo-Saxon *Eostre*, from the existence of forms such as *ôstarun* in southeastern Old High German dialects. Grimm does not, however, explain how this southeastern area of 'Easter' terms comes to be separated from the other area of 'Easter' terms, namely England, by a band of terms deriving from Latin *pascha*. Frings and Müller (1966-68: 1.38-9) address this issue, arguing that *pascha* forms originate from borrowing of the Latin term within the bishopric of Cologne. These forms then spread from Cologne, and this particularly accounts for their presence in Frisia, Saxony and Scandinavia. This leaves the exact status of Old English *ēastre* and Old High German *ôstarun* somewhat unclear, but it would appear that Frings and Müller envisage these as reflecting a traditional festival name (whether derived from a deity or not) in England and some parts of the Continent.

This might, then, suggest that some of the *pascha* forms mask the existence of a festival (and perhaps a goddess) that was spread over an area from southeastern Germany to England. The result is that we have a claim not unlike that of Grimm, but focussing on the idea of a pre-Christian festival, and leaving the possible relationship of this festival to a deity out of the picture. Green (2000: 351-3) builds on this idea, suggesting that an Old High German festival-name *ôstarun* was developed as a term for the Christian festival due to the influence of Old English *ēastre* in a Christian context: he sees this as one of a number of terms that can plausibly be attributed to the influence of English Christian terminology resulting from the presence of Anglo-Saxon clerics in Germany (349-56). There is, however, no reason why such influence should not operate in the absence of a pre-existing Old High German festival name. Helm (1950: 9) argues that *ēastre* is unlikely to have been loaned into Old High German in the Anglo-Saxon missionary context, on the grounds that *ôstarun* was not used in the main area of the mission. Yet the area of usage of *ôstarun*, as Frings and Müller (1966-68: 1.38 and map 6) point out, includes the diocese of Mainz. We know, moreover, that Boniface – who operated in Hesse and Thuringia and was ultimately made bishop of Mainz – repeatedly requested copies of works of Bede in his letters to individuals in Northumbria (Tangl 1916: nos 75, 76 and 91). His successor Lull also requested copies of works by Bede (Tangl 1916: nos 126 and 127), and Petersohn (1966: 238-9) has connected these requests with some of the earliest manuscripts of Bede's works, including the Bückeburg fragment of *De Temporum Ratione*. McKitterick (2004: 94), however, points out that Lull's book requests did not include *De Temporum Ratione*, and suggests that it might 'be feasible to think in terms of a copy [of *De Temporum Ratione*] being sent to the continent earlier'. Even if Bede himself were responsible (which seems unlikely: see p. 69) for spreading the use of the term *ēastre* in Anglo-Saxon England, then, it is by no means implausible that Anglo-Saxon activities within and around the see of Mainz should bring with them the term *ēastre* and cause it to be adopted in this area. This would support the suggestion of missionary influence by Sermon (2008: 337). We need not, therefore, assume that there was either a festival or a goddess spread across England and the Continent – but this does not mean that we should discount Bede's claims for a goddess worshipped in early Anglo-Saxon England.

4. Eostre: Pan-Germanic Goddess or 'Etymological Fancy'

The etymology of *Eostre*

If there are problems with the claims for a continental equivalent of Eostre, there are also problems associated with the etymological discussions of her name on which interpretations of her role and function have usually been based. Grimm's view that she was a goddess associated with the dawn depends on the fact that the sun rises in the East. The name *Eostre* is etymologically related to the word *east*, which has cognates in most Germanic languages, and this prompted Grimm's interpretation. This etymological argument was developed further by Helm (1950: 9), who considered the etymological connections of *Eostre* beyond the Germanic languages. He pointed out that Latin *Aurora*, Greek 'Hώς and Sanskrit *Ushas* (all meaning 'dawn', and also used as the names of goddesses) can all be related to the same root as that which appears in the word *east*. On this basis, he suggests that there is some evidence for an Indo-European goddess of the dawn, whose Germanic reflex is Eostre. Given that she gives her name to a month, however, he sees the Germanic goddess as relating to the dawning of the year (that is, Spring) rather than the dawning of each day (Helm 1950: 9).

This interpretation of Eostre as a Spring goddess has been strangely influential, given the lack of really clear evidence to support it. Both sceptics and believers often refer to her as a Spring goddess, and this leads to some preposterous situations, as when Knobloch (1959: 31-4) argues against the existence of Eostre on the grounds that there is a lack of strong etymological evidence for her connection with the Spring. This is clearly no argument against the goddess at all – Knobloch ably demonstrates the weakness of the supposed connection with Spring, but this connection is, after all, only one scholarly interpretation of Eostre's name. The weaknesses of modern claims as to her role and function are not an argument against the existence of Eostre; and in fact there is a rather more plausible interpretation of her name, which we will now consider.

The name *Eostre* has, as discussed above, been considered to be related to the Old English word *ēast* ('east'). Similarly, the form *Austriahenae* has been taken to derive from a root **austra*, meaning 'east' (Neumann 1987: 109) – but while Old English *ēast* and **austra* are clearly related, they are not etymologically identical. Both *Eostre* and *Austriahenae* include an

55

/r/ after the sequence /st/, which forms part of the stem of Old English *ēastre*, but which is absent in Old English *ēast* and, indeed, in other West Germanic cognates of this word, such as Old High German *ōst* and Old Saxon *ôst* (Schützeichel 2006: under *ōst*; Holthausen 1954: under *ôst*). This /r/ requires some etymological explanation, if we are to have a full understanding of the development of the names *Eostre* and *Austriahenae*. One possible explanation is the now traditional connection of *ēastre* with Latin *aurora* and other related Indo-European roots. According to this interpretation, we have a root **aus-r*, with /t/ subsequently intruding. This is not the only possible etymology, however.

A glance at the entry for *ēast* in Bosworth-Toller might give the impression that this /r/ is a remnant of an earlier form of the word *ēast*. Bosworth-Toller identifies *ēast* as a strong masculine noun, and apparently considers this noun to be cognate with the Old Norse strong masculine noun *austr*. This implies perfectly regular developments of a Primitive Germanic **austaz* to Old Norse *austr* and Old English *ēast*; but a closer inspection of the evidence suggests that Bosworth-Toller has been led astray by the resemblance between the Old English and the Old Norse words. In fact, a careful examination of the evidence for Old English *ēast* does not produce any indication whatsoever that it was a noun. A quick test for this is to check for inflected forms of the word: if it were indeed a strong masculine noun, we should normally expect to find a genitive singular form **ēastes* and a dative singular **ēaste*. Given that 'the East' is by definition singular, we should not expect to find plural forms of this noun, but if we did, we would anticipate seeing nominative and accusative plural **ēastas*, genitive plural **ēasta* and dative plural **ēastum*. A search of *DOEC* allows us to check for these forms in a corpus containing at least one version of almost every text composed in Old English that is still extant. The results of such a search (using the 'simple search' facility to search for each of the terms listed in the table as a 'whole word') are given in Table 3.

	Singular		Plural	
	Expected form	Occurrences	Expected form	Occurrences
Nominative	*ēast*	325	*ēastas*	0
Accusative	*ēast*		*ēastas*	
Genitive	*ēastes*	0	*ēasta*	2
Dative	*ēaste*	2	*ēastum*	0

Table 3. Occurrences of *ēast* in *DOEC*.

These results are startlingly biased towards the uninflected form of the putative noun *ēast* – so much so that we might reasonably question whether the two instances each of *ēaste* and *ēasta* actually represent inflected forms of a noun *ēast* at all. Of the two instances of *ēaste*, one (Sawyer 364) is an instance of the compound adjective *ēasteweard* with the two elements written as if they were two separate words (not an uncommon occurrence in Anglo-Saxon manuscripts). The second (Sawyer 680) can probably be best understood as a reduced form of the related adverb *ēastan* ('from the east') with loss of final /n/ and reduction of the unstressed /ɑ/ to schwa (based on the reconstruction of the bounds in Crawford 1922: 75-80); *DOE*, on the other hand, appears to regard this as simply an alternative spelling of *ēast* (under *ēast*). The two examples of *ēasta*, both from the Lindisfarne Gospels gloss, are clearly both examples of this adverb in a reduced form with loss of final /n/, as they both translate Latin *ab oriente* ('from the east') (Stevenson and Waring 1854-65: 1.81 and 3.117).

We have found, then, no evidence for any of the inflected forms we might expect of a strong masculine noun *ēast*. The other test that we should perform is to examine the 325 instances of the form *ēast* to see whether or not any of them can be interpreted as nouns. An exhaustive listing and discussion of this material is clearly not practicable here, but happily the *Dictionary of Old English* project has already completed its section on words beginning with <e>, and this analysis has therefore already been performed by the project team. They have apparently found no examples of *ēast* used as a noun, and they treat it simply as an adverb – and the example quotations they give amply bear out this reading of the situation. We have no reason to believe that there was a strong masculine noun *ēast* ('the east') in Old English.

What, then, of the Old Norse *austr*, which is listed in Bosworth-Toller as a relative of the supposed noun *ēast*? There is rather stronger evidence for the existence of an Old Norse noun *austr*, since a genitive singular form *austrs* appears in the phrase *til austrs* ('to the east') and a dative singular form in the phrase *í austri* ('in the east'). It seems possible that the invention of the noun *ēast* in Bosworth-Toller was prompted by the existence of what was taken to be an Old Norse cognate for the Old English word. The similarity is strengthened by the fact that the Old Norse word *austr* is usually used adverbially, as is *ēast* in Old English: the inflected forms appear to be fossilised remnants of its existence as a noun. Indeed, given that Old High German texts provide evidence for a rare adjective *ōstar* beside a more common adverb *ōstar* (Schützeichel 2006: under *ōstar¹* and *ōstar²*), we might argue that an adjective in the common ancestor of these languages, which could behave as a noun, had largely developed into an adverb by the period in which most Old Norse texts were produced, with a few conventional phrases retaining inflected forms that indicate its development from an adjective/noun.

It is, however, clear that the adjective/noun *austr* could not be a cognate of an Old English noun *ēast*, since the /r/ of *austr* is in fact thematic; that is, it is not simply the nominative singular ending, but forms part of the stem of the word, appearing also in the genitive and dative singular forms. It is normal for the Germanic nominative singular inflexion which appears in Old Norse as -*r* (as in *dagr* 'day') to appear in Old English as a zero inflexion (as in *dæg* 'day', which is a cognate of *dagr*); but the evidence that the /r/ of *austr* is thematic shows that this sound is not simply derived from the Germanic nominative singular inflexion. We should therefore expect this /r/ to feature in some form in the Old English cognate of *austr*, if there is one. A parallel case demonstrates the point: Old Norse *eitr* ('poison'; genitive singular *eitrs*) corresponds not to an Old English noun **āt* (genitive singular **ātes*), but to Old English *āttor* ('poison'; genitive singular *āttres*). We should therefore expect an Old English **ēastor* as a cognate of Old Norse *austr*: and such a word could well prove helpful in elucidating the etymology of *Eostre* (and *Austriahenae*), as it includes the thematic /r/ which is present in these names.

Eostre and place-names

The conjectural Old English word **ēastor* has been invoked (quite independently of any discussion of *Eostre*) to explain a small number of English place-names. Neumann (1987: 109) also notes this element as an etymological relative of the name *Austriahenae*. Smith (1956: 145) identified **ēastor* as the first element of the place-names *Eastrea* (Cambridgeshire) and *Eastry* (Kent). Ekwall (1960: under *ēast* and *Eastrington*) also considered *Eastrington* (East Riding of Yorkshire) to contain this element, and Mills (2003: under *Eastrington*) agrees with Ekwall on this point. According to Smith, **ēastor* 'is probably an old form, which became obsolete very early in OE' (Smith 1956: 145). Smith probably based this view on the lack of attestations of *ēastor* as an independent word, which suggests that it had fallen out of use in the early Anglo-Saxon period, before significant quantities of textual material in Old English began to be produced. Some caution is required in identifying place-names containing the element *ēastor*, however, as there is also a comparative adjective *ēastra* (meaning, according to *DOE*, under *ēastra*, 'situated in / lying toward the east, eastern'). No positive form of this adjective is certainly attested, and the senses in which it is used suggest that no positive form need have existed. This adjective appears frequently in references to landmarks in charter bounds (see the listing in *DOE*, under *ēastra*), and is also attested as a place-name element in the names of settlements such as Asterton in Shropshire and Easterton in Wiltshire (Mills 2003: under *Asterton* and *Easterton*). It is difficult, therefore, to distinguish instances of *ēastra* in place-names from instances of *ēastor*. The modern forms of place-names may be a poor guide, as various linguistic changes can obscure the Old English origins of such forms, and the presence of /r/ in a modern form of a place-name such as *Eastrea* or *Eastrington* could be attributed to either *ēastra* or *ēastor*. Careful consideration of the earliest available attestations of place-names is therefore necessary if we are to distinguish accurately between *ēastra* and *ēastor* place-names. Table 4 (overleaf) details the early attestations of place-names which have been identified as *ēastor* place-names.

The early forms of *Eastry* clearly show the presence of the vowel /o/ in the second syllable of *eastor*, demonstrating that this is unlikely to be an instance of *ēastra*: where *ēastra* is spelt with a vowel graph between <t> and <r>, it is always <e> (*DOE*: under *ēastra*). There is more room for doubt with the other place-names, where the earliest forms do not demonstrate the existence of /o/ as the original vowel of the second syllable of the word. Nevertheless, early forms of the name of Eastry in Kent provide sufficient evidence to suggest that *ēastor* probably did exist as a word during the period of formation of this place-name, and we can reasonably relate this word to the name *Eostre*. It would, of course, be possible to make a case for Eostre deriving her name from the comparative form *ēastra*, but the form *ēastor* seems, on balance, to be more likely, given that, in *De Temporum Ratione*, the month-name

59

Date	Document	Eastry, Kent	Eastrea, Cambridgeshire	Eastrington, East Riding of Yorkshire
788 AD	Sawyer 128	*Eastrgena*		
811 AD	Sawyer 1264	*Easterege* (x2) *Eostorege* (x2) *Eosterege* (x1) *Eosterge* (x1)		
805x832 AD	Sawyer 1500	*Eastorege*		
825x832 AD	Sawyer 1268	*Eastræge*		
959 AD	Sawyer 681			*Eastringatun*
966 AD (but likely to be a late eleventh- or early twelfth-century forgery: see Roffe 1995: 102-8)	Sawyer 741		*Estrey*	
mid to late twelfth century (see Blake 1962: xlviii-xlix)	*Liber Eliensis* (Blake 1962: 132)		*Estereie*	

Table 4. Early attestations of *ēastor* place-names.

clearly has a back vowel (spelt <u> in most of the early manuscripts) in the second syllable. This agrees better with *ēastor* than with *ēastra*.

Eostre and personal names

The element *ēastor* does not appear to be confined to place-names. This word, or the related festival name, appears as a prototheme in the name *Easterwine*, borne by a seventh-century abbot of Bede's monastery of Wearmouth-Jarrow (*PASE*: under *Eosterwine 1*). The same name appears three times in the Durham *Liber Vitae*, where the name *Aestorhild* also appears (Gerchow 1988: 380). The latter name is very probably the ancestor of the Middle English name *Estrild* (Seltén 1979: 2.80-1). There is somewhat more evidence on the Continent: Reichert (1987-90: 2.472) lists a number of names evidenced in this context, such as *Austrechild*, *Austrighysel*, *Austrovald* and *Ostrulf* (see also under *Austrechild*, *Austrighysel*, *Austrovald*, *Ostrulf*). Sermon's suggestion that *Easterwine* should be understood as meaning 'Eostre's friend' is unacceptable on linguistic grounds (the name element is *ēastor* not the feminine form used for the goddess's name) and fails to account for the evidence outside Old English (2008: 334). The name *Eostre* is, then, perhaps not

60

unrelated to traditions of naming people and places. And we have seen such interlocking traditions of divine names with localities and personal names before – in the evidence for matron cults.

Eostre and the matrons

It appears, then, that we can link the forms *Eostre* and *Austriahenae* on etymological grounds, and that there are similarities between the nature of the name *Eostre* and the naming patterns of matrons such as the Austriahenae. This does not, however, imply that Eostre developed from the Austriahenae, or that there was an ancestral link of some sort between the worshippers of the Austriahenae and the worshippers of Eostre. The fact that Bede refers to a pre-Christian festival *modranect* ('night of mothers'), which does suggest a development from the cults of matrons (Meaney 1985: 5-6; North 1997: 227), need not indicate that Eostre is part of that development: indeed, the dating of *modranect* in December, as against Eostre's association with April, tends to demonstrate that Eostre need have no direct connection with the matron cults. Yet the fact that Bede's account of *modranect* can be to some extent confirmed by the Romano-Germanic votive inscriptions to matrons does at least indicate that we should not be too quick to dismiss the other evidence he provides for Anglo-Saxon deities.

It has been suggested that Eostre might in fact be a group of deities, rather than an individual. Helm (1950: 10) argued that the fact that the word 'Easter' is very commonly used in the plural in Old English and in Old High German might indicate that it developed from a group of goddesses. These he connected with the *idisi* ('ladies') who have often been invoked as collective goddesses from the continental Germanic area, perhaps cognate with the *dísir* of Scandinavian tradition, producing a vision of the name 'Easter' developing from a festival of 'Frühlings*idisi*' ('Spring-*idisi*'; Helm 1950: 10). Quite apart from the lack of evidence for uses of 'east' and it relatives and derivatives as words for 'dawn' or 'Spring' in the Germanic languages, there are also considerable problems with the idea that there were collective goddesses (or semi-goddesses) termed *idisi* in continental Germanic-speaking societies. The word *idis/itis* has an Old English cognate *ides*, which is rare, and usually applied to human women, although Grendel's mother in *Beowulf* is also described as an *ides* (Meaney 1979: 23-5). The Old High German *itis* and Old Saxon *idis* are also very rare, and the identification of this word as a term for goddesses seems to rest mainly on two points: first, the word is used to refer to a group of women in the *First Merseburg Charm* who are often identified as supernatural women (Murdoch 2004a: 62, for instance, identifies them as valkyries and seems to gloss the term *idisi* as meaning 'valkyries'; Eis 1964a: 64-5 attempts to connect these figures with the cult of matrons on the basis of glossarial evidence, but the use of *itis* as a gloss for *matrona* could readily be explained on the basis that *itis* means nothing more than 'lady'; Meaney 1979: 23 is more cautious in arguing simply that these are not normal women); and secondly, the word has been taken to be related to the Old Norse term *dísir*, which is undoubtedly used to refer to collective female goddesses in some Old Norse texts (Damico 1984: 68-72; Simek 2002: 115-17). There are problems with both of these points. The women of the *First Merseburg Charm* are depicted fastening and unfastening bonds, and in some way obstructing an army, but this need not imply that they are doing so by supernatural means, let alone that they are themselves supernatural (Eis 1949: 38). It is true that the *Second Merseburg Charm* mentions the names of a number of deities (Eis 1949: 38), and, like the *First Merseburg Charm* it is a historiola (that is, a charm in which a narrative is employed that in some way represents or symbolises the achievement of the desired outcome of the charm); but this need hardly mean that both charms involve deities. The relationship between the terms *idisi* and *dísir* is, if anything, still more problematic. There is no regular set of sound changes that could account for these forms as developing from a single Proto-Germanic word, and, as De Vries (1977: under *dís*) rightly points out, there is evidence from personal names that demonstrates the existence of a proto-Germanic root for *dís* independent of *ides*. It seems unlikely that *ides* and *dís* are cognate, and we should therefore be wary of attempting to equate matrons with *dísir* or to establish the existence of extra-Scandinavian *dísir* cults on the basis of the term *ides*.

The attempts to identify common Germanic goddesses may, to a large extent, be misguided. It seems reasonable to accept Bede's evidence for *modranect* as an indication that some sort of cult similar to that of the matrons continued to exist in at least some part of early Anglo-Saxon England. This, however, is a far cry from suggesting that a single, specific set of collective female deities were worshipped across Germanic-speaking societies in England, parts of the Continent, and Scandinavia, with a common term *ides/idis/dís* to denote these deities. The evidence for matron cults discussed in the previous chapter actually speaks against this pan-Germanising approach to the evidence. If there is one absolutely characteristic feature of the cults of matrons it is that they are fundamentally local. While we might identify matrons as a broad type of deity, we should not lose sight of the fact that their epithets, and the ways in which devotees referred to them in differing geographical and social contexts, seek to locate them in relation to tribal and sub-tribal social groups and their localities.

The local quality of matron cults clearly seems relevant to the way we interpret the Austriahenae. The etymology of their name, as we have seen, supports an interpretation of them as 'eastern matrons'. Given the importance of small-scale social groups in matron-epithets, this might mean something like 'matrons belonging to an eastern group of people'. We cannot hope to determine exactly how such a group might have been defined as eastern, and who might have been involved in this identification. Some broad outlines can, however, be ascertained. The Austriahenae are evidenced by a very large number of inscriptions, found in a single locality. The quantity of inscriptions can be compared with the numbers found at the cult-sites of Nehalennia, where there were very probably temple buildings (Hondius-Crone 1955: 11-19; Stuart and Bogaers 2001: 43; Stuart 2003), and with the altars to the Vacallinehae found in association with a temple complex at Pesch in the Eifel (Garman 2008: 53-4; see map on p. 42 for location). Even less frequently attested matrons have sometimes been found in association with sanctuaries (Derks 1991: 245; Garman 2008: 54-6). Thus, although no temple or sanctuary site has been discovered in the area, Kolbe's (1960: 51) view that there was probably a cult centre of the Austriahenae in the vicinity of the findsite near Morken-Harff is persuasive. This suggests that the findsite is within the area usually inhabited by the worshippers of the Austriahenae, and we might therefore, as discussed in the previous chapter, expect that the name *Austriahenae* refers to a relatively small-scale group and their locality. This is confirmed by the fact that a votive inscription from the Morken-Harff findsite also refers to the *Austriates*, evidently a group-name (Kolbe 1960: 58; Roymans 1990: 50). This group name may well relate in some way to local social geography, and we should therefore not see the name *Austriahenae* as related to the idea of migration from east of the Rhine, but rather as relating to local positioning in relation to other groups or areas in the region.

Eostre as local goddess

This portrait of the cult of the Austriahenae, incomplete as it necessarily is, may also provide us with some clues to the nature of the cult of Eostre. The fact that early Anglo-Saxon place-names clearly testify to the use of the term **ēastor* in referring to local areas (as in the case of Eastry), and perhaps also local groups (as in the case of Eastrington) would seem to support an interpretation of Eostre as a goddess associated with such a group and/or area. It is not implausible to suggest that the names of Eostre and of the Austriahenae are etymologically similar not because they are directly related to one another, but because they reflect similar broad patterns of naming practices in the early Germanic languages. In other words, these are deities with local importance, whose names developed in parallel ways to refer to an area or a group that was in some way identified as eastern.

This is, in many ways, an obvious way to understand Eostre: and in fact it does away with the need to make special arguments for a relationship between words related to 'east' and the idea of dawn or even Spring. There is, in fact, little reason to suppose that the Germanic languages usually treated 'east' and its relatives and derivatives as related to dawn. Latin uses the word *oriens* to mean both 'east' and 'dawning', and, as noted above, terms like the Latin *aurora* ('dawn') are ultimately etymologically related to the word 'east' in the Germanic languages. This is, however, a very ancient connection, which suggests the recognition of a semantic connection between the words for 'east' and 'dawn' in a stratum of the development of the Indo-European languages that pre-dates Proto-Germanic. We are not, therefore, obliged to believe that such a connection existed in the Germanic languages.

Locating Eostre

The early forms of the name of Eastry in Kent listed above (p. 60) are also important for the evidence they provide about early Kentish spellings of the initial diphthong of the word **ēastor*. There are a number of spellings with <eo>, alongside the more common <ea> spellings. As Shaw (2008: 102-3) notes, Bede's preferred spelling for this diphthong in his *Historia Ecclesiastica* is <ea>, but he uses <eo> on occasion in the name of Eadbald of Kent (616-40), probably reflecting the orthography of his source or sources. This would be consistent with the evidence for Kentish <eo> spellings in the early attestations of Eastry. There is, however, also evidence for the use of <eo> spellings in some southerly parts of Northumbria in the eighth century (Shaw 2008: 101-4). This suggests that Bede's <eo> spelling of *Eostre* is likely to reflect his use of a written source from outside his own locality – but it does not allow us to pin down the origins of this source with any precision. It is possible that written sources from many parts of England would have used <eo> spellings, not just Kentish sources: for most areas we simply do not have the data to determine this.

Nevertheless, there are some other possible hints that Eostre might be associated with Kent, and perhaps even with Eastry specifically. It is probable that Bede was using a written source for his Anglo-Saxon month-names, and we should not be particularly surprised to find Bede obtaining such sources from Kent: we know that Bede was to receive material for the *Historia Ecclesiastica* from Kent (Brooks 1989: 59), and he may therefore already have had contacts in Kent when he was composing *De Temporum Ratione*. As Herren (1998) has shown, moreover, the early eighth century saw considerable interest in Graeco-Roman mythology and its correspondences with native pagan mythology in southern Anglo-Saxon centres, including Canterbury. Such interests would certainly be consonant with the production of a listing of Anglo-Saxon month-names in relation to their Roman equivalents, as in chapter 15 of *De Temporum Ratione*. These considerations suggest that Kent is a plausible area to look for Bede's source of information on the Anglo-Saxon month-names, although they certainly do not rule out other areas in southern England.

On the other hand, one piece of evidence could be seen as speaking against a Kentish source, namely the month-name *rugern* (which appears to be connected with the name of the cereal crop rye) mentioned in the dating formula of the laws of Wihtræd of Kent (690-725 AD): this seems to be a Kentish month-name that does not form part of Bede's sequence (Weinhold 1869: 3; Liebermann 1903-16: 1.12). On the other hand,

Ashley (1928: 131) argues that Kent is unlikely to have been a major rye growing area, and therefore suggests that *rugern* reflects the usage of the area in which the laws were promulgated, taking *Berghamstyde* in Wihtræd's laws to refer to Berkhamsted (presumably Little Berkhamsted in Hertfordshire, rather than Great Berkhamsted, as the former is much nearer the border with Essex, a county which he regards as a plausible area for widespread rye cultivation). There have, however, been other identifications for *Berghamstyde*, prompted by the difficulties of locating a Kentish council in Hertfordshire: with Barham in Kent, near Canterbury, and with Bearsted in Kent, near Maidstone (Liebermann 1903-16: 3.25). The former identification is impossible, since the first attestation of the name is in the form *Bioraham* in a charter of 799 (Ekwall 1960: under *Barham*; Sawyer 155). At this early date, we would not expect spellings lacking the <g> that appears in the form *Berghamstyde*. On the other hand, Bersted in Sussex has been adduced as evidence that *Berghamstyde* could become *Bearsted*, since in this case there is persuasive evidence for the reduction of the second element *hām* in an original **Beorghāmstede* (Liebermann 1903-16: 3.25; Ekwall 1960: under *Bersted*; Mills 2003: under *Bersted*). The identification with Bearsted near Maidstone is accepted by both Mills (2003: under *Bearsted*) and Ekwall (1960: under *Bearsted*), presumably on the basis of the development seen in the name of Bersted in Sussex. If we are satisfied that Wihtræd cannot have held a council at Bersted in Sussex, Bearsted in Kent certainly seems to be a plausible location for it. This location, just to the east of Maidstone, lies well to the west of Canterbury, and outside the earliest Kentish districts (on which, see below). It therefore seems quite possible that *rugern* represents a western Kentish usage, whereas *Eostre*, if Bede received his month-list from Canterbury, would be an eastern Kentish form. The location of Wihtræd's council is likely to remain a matter for debate, and patterns of rye cultivation in the early Anglo-Saxon period are neither well enough attested nor sufficiently regionally homogenous to allow firm conclusions to be drawn from a connection with rye cultivation (Green 1994: 84-6; Rackham 1994a). Given the several uncertainties, we would be unwise to dismiss the possibility that the month-name *rugern* reflects a regional variation of usage within Kent itself, and we should not therefore see this name as strong evidence against a Kentish source for Bede's month-names.

4. Eostre: Pan-Germanic Goddess or 'Etymological Fancy'

Eastry itself is clearly an early place-name. Quite apart from the fact that the term **ēastor* appears to have been lost from Old English early on, the second element **gē* 'district' is, according to Gelling, 'a word believed to have become obsolete at an early date in Old English' (1988: 123). The name appears originally to have been applied to one of the four regions forming the original core of the kingdom of Kent (Brooks 1989: 73), and Eastry – like the other **gē* names of eastern Kent, *Sturry* and *Lyminge* – is the site of significant early Anglo-Saxon cemetery finds (Hawkes 1979: 81; Behr 2000). It also appears to have been a royal estate centre, and the location of an early Anglo-Saxon church (Riddler 2004: 26; Carder 2004). Indeed, Hawkes suggests that Eastry, Sturry and Lyminge may well have been 'operating as royal district capitals from a very early date indeed, at least from the reign of Ethelbert and probably from the very beginning of established kingship in Kent' (Hawkes 1979: 81).

While there is no direct evidence for a conception of the inhabitants of the region of Eastry as a distinct social grouping, *Sturry* and *Lyminge* can plausibly be related to the terms *Burhwaraweald* and *Limenwaraweald*, which imply groups known as the **Burhwara* ('inhabitants of the area of the *burh* [=Canterbury]') and **Limenwara* ('inhabitants of the area of the river Lympne') (Brooks 1989: 73). It seems quite probable that the inhabitants of the region of Eastry could be termed the **Ēastorwara* ('inhabitants of the eastern area'). Such a local social grouping, below the level of kingdom or tribe, offers a plausible analogue for the groupings within which the cults of matrons evidently operated. None of this proves any specific connection between Eostre and Eastry, of course, but this does make a case for the existence in pre-Christian England of relatively small-scale social groupings which quite possibly had their own local, group-specific goddesses – and Eostre could well be just such a goddess.

Sub-tribal groupings

The regions of Eastry, Sturry and Lyminge are far from unique: such sub-tribal local groupings can be discerned in various Anglo-Saxon place-names elsewhere. In Essex a group of **gē* names appears in a number of contiguous parishes (Margaretting, Ingatestone, Fryerning and Mountnessing, together with one outlier, Ingrave) covering an area of approximately 40 square kilometres.[2] Blair (1989: 102) has argued plausibly that the modern county name *Surrey*, whose second element was also *gē, may once have referred to a rather smaller area, perhaps more comparable with the areas associated with the Kentish *gē names. The two other *gē place-names known to me, *Ely* (Cambridgeshire) and *Vange* (Essex), are both, as their names suggest, in fenland, and may therefore have formed rather smaller than usual self-contained districts, defined by the surrounding fens.

The place-name element *gē is not the only indication of such local territories. Another group of contiguous, interrelated parishes, like the *gē parishes in Essex discussed above, are the Rodings, also in Essex, covering an area of approximately 50 square kilometres.[3] The name *Roding* appears to derive from an Old English name *Hroþingas* ('followers/family of Hroþa'), and the area defined by the outer boundary of these parishes has been interpreted as the sort of region that 'one would expect a well organized, self-contained community living under an economy of subsistence and exchange to have occupied' (Bassett 1989a: 21). To this we can add that such communities may well have continued to enact distinct identities within larger kingdoms, as the survival of Eastry as a Domesday lathe suggests (Lawson 2004; but see also the caution in Campbell 1979: 48). It seems reasonable to suppose that in pre-Christian times such communities had their own specific deities.

The Anglo-Saxon term *gē, moreover, does not appear to have been unique. Documents on the Continent also record this term in the cognate form *gau*, and in a number of instances place-names containing the element *gau* are stated to refer to *pagi*: for instance, the monastery of St Gall records (Wartmann 1981) grants of land in 775 AD 'in pago Durgauvia' (no. 76), in 807 AD 'in pago Durgaugense' (no. 193), in 812 AD 'in pago, quod dicitur Nibulgauia' (no. 210), and in 815 AD 'in pago Brisicauginse' (no. 214). This indicates not only the comparatively rich system of *gau* regions in the wider area (compared with the rather patchy evidence for England), but also suggests that *gau* may have functioned more or less as an equivalent to the Roman term *pagus*, a term that often appears to designate a local, sub-tribal socio-political and religious grouping in Roman accounts of the Celts and Germani (Roymans 1990: 19-21).

4. Eostre: Pan-Germanic Goddess or 'Etymological Fancy'

Month-name and festival

This analysis of Eostre has implications for our understanding of the name of the Christian festival of Easter. If Eostre can be understood within the framework of locally-defined goddesses associated with sub-tribal socio-political groupings, then this raises questions about the relationship of the month connected with her name to the festival of Easter. While some scholars have attempted elaborate reappraisals of the relationship, that discount the goddess and establish links instead with white baptismal garments and the dawn (Knobloch 1959), or with a supposed term for baptism (Udolph 1999), I would suggest a return to the view that the Christian festival simply took its name from the month within which it most commonly fell. Anglo-Saxon Christians appear to have been willing to make use of ostensibly pagan names for the days of the week – and I have argued elsewhere that this may well have been a product of learned, Christian environments, rather than a tenacious hangover from the pre-Christian past (Shaw 2007: 395-400). We need not be unduly surprised to find the name of the month coming to be associated with – and ultimately applied to – the festival that was, for an early medieval Christian, one of the religious and social highlights not only of the month itself, but of the entire year.

Seen in this light, one might suspect that Bede in fact gave Eostre her big break, that his treatment of her month in *De Temporum Ratione* – one of the essential ecclesiastical textbooks of the early Middle Ages, and one whose early dissemination appears to have involved very substantial copying on the Continent, perhaps in part by insular missionaries (Jones 1943: 142; Wallis 1999: lxxxvi-lxxxvii) – was instrumental in the spread of the name of the festival and month to the Continent. His discussion of the month-name in *De Temporum Ratione* is unlikely, however, to have been key to the spread of the term within England. He indicates that the month-name had already been re-analysed as relating to the name of the Christian festival, stating that it 'is now translated "Paschal month"' (Wallis 1999: 54). This strongly suggests that the festival name had already spread, along with the month-name, across England. It seems possible that the spread of the name for the festival and month was more or less of a piece with the spread of Christianisation within England, and that processes of Christianisation smoothed away some of the local variety in English month-names that survives in the West Saxon *blydmonaþ* where Bede gives the name *hredmonath* (on local variation in Old English month-names, see pp. 94-6), and in the name *rugern* (on which see pp. 65-6). On the Continent, we get a glimpse of the sort of variety that might once have been the case in pre-Christian England in the diverse sets of month-names recorded in late medieval calendars (Weinhold 1869). If Eostre were a Kentish deity, as suggested above, this would certainly not be inconsistent with such a spread of the month-name via Christianisation.

Conclusion

The answer to the question posed in the title of this chapter turns out to be 'neither': Eostre is probably not 'an etymological fancy', nor yet a pan-Germanic goddess. The picture we have developed looks rather different. We have found evidence for parallel naming practices in an early Anglo-Saxon goddess and a group of matrons. This need not surprise us, given the considerable similarities between the naming practices of the various early Germanic dialects: the basic patterns of name formation in the Germanic languages appear to have quite ancient origins. However, more than a parallel of naming practice, the specific name-element involved suggests a general parallel in terms of the basic structure of these two cults. The association with a topographical term suggests that the pattern of numerous, tightly localised cults visible in the Romano-Germanic votive inscriptions may be similar to patterns in early Anglo-Saxon England – though we have much less evidence for these. We cannot push this very far, as ultimately our picture of Anglo-Saxon pre-Christian religious life must rest on the evidence from Anglo-Saxon contexts. We can hardly expect that this will ever be anything more that partial, however, and the evidence discussed here suggests that the evidence of the Romano-Germanic votive inscriptions may at least provide some useful broad models, although we should be cautious about seeking detailed evidence in this material.

The other important conclusion to draw from this exploration of Eostre is that we have reason to think that a key feature in her individual construction is geographically and perhaps socially defined. The previous work on her, in common with much work on pre-Christian deities, has tended to focus on the idea that she should have a function or area of expertise: either the dawn or the Spring. This notion of function casts a long shadow over studies of pre-Christian deities, with numerous attempts to identify or characterise the special areas of activity of particular deities or groupings of deities (see, for example, the characterisation of Odin in Davidson 1972 and the treatment of Vanir and Æsir roles in DuBois 1999: 54-8) and even general patterns of function into which deities can be grouped. The most obvious example of the latter approach is the Dumézilian tripartite function model, which can broadly be seen as categorising deities according to the functions of rulership, warfare and fertility (but to be fair to Dumézil, we should note that he himself recognises that deities can have overlapping functions; see Dumézil 1973: 36-7). Derks (1998: 77-81) has pointed out the considerable difficulties involved in applying such models to late Roman votive inscriptions of the Rhine area, and this analysis of Eostre should caution us against indiscriminate applications of the idea of function to Anglo-Saxon deities. Eostre – and perhaps, therefore, other Anglo-Saxon deities as well – appears to have been principally defined by her relationship to a social and geographical grouping. If they believed that she had a specialist function or functions, we have no evidence for this belief – and the etymological connections of her name suggest that her worshippers saw her geographical and social relationship with them as more central than any functions she may have had.

5

Hreda

The discussion of Eostre in the previous chapter may well provide some indications of possible ways of understanding the other goddess of Bede's *De Temporum Ratione*, Hreda. The importance of locality and social groupings at local level are potentially important here, as is the recognition that pre-Christian Anglo-Saxon deities need not have been primarily defined in terms of the modern conception of function. We should be wary of starting from the assumption that Hreda's name will indicate a particular sphere of activity or influence on her part; and this may allow us to explore fruitful new directions. To begin with, however, we have to wrestle with some fundamental linguistic issues surrounding the name *Hreda*.

The name *Eostre* raises various problems, discussed in the previous chapter, but in one respect it is relatively simple: apart from *ēast* and its derivatives, it is the only word in the extant corpus of Old English beginning with the sequence <eost> or <east>. We do not, therefore, have to consider several possible candidates for related words in attempting to establish an etymology.

Unfortunately, we face a much more complex set of problems in identifying possible etymological relatives of the name *Hreda*. Not only are there more Old English words with a similar pattern; there are also more possible identifications of the Old English phonemes represented by the form *Hreda*. The initial <hr> is unproblematic, but the <d> presents difficulties. It could, of course, represent the Old English phoneme /d/, but it could also represent /ð/. Early manuscripts of Bede's *Historia Ecclesiastica Gentis Anglorum* ('Ecclesiastical History of the English People') suggest that Bede used <d> to represent Old English /d/ and /ð/ (Blair and Mynors 1959: 20). In seeking words that may be etymologically related to the name *Hreda*, therefore, we have to consider words with initial /hr/ followed by a vowel (probably a front vowel) followed by either /ð/ or /d/. Some searches of *DOEC* reveal a number of possibilities: *hræd/hræð/hreð* 'quick', *hrēod* 'reed', *hrēða* 'goatskin', *hrēðan* 'to rejoice', and *hrēð* 'victory, glory'.

The -*a* ending of *Hreda* is unlikely to be helpful in elucidating the etymology of the name *Hreda*. In dealing with the monothematic Old English names of human women, Bede usually incorporates them into his *Historia Ecclesiastica Gentis Anglorum* as first declension Latin nouns: hence *Acha* (book 3, chapter 6), *Aebbæ* (book 4, chapters 19 and 25), *Bebba/Bebbae* (book 3, chapters 6 and 16), *Bercta/Berctae* (book 1, chapter 25; book 2, chapter 5), *Eabae* (book 4, chapter 13), *Fara* (book 3, chapter 8), *Tatae* (book 2, chapter 9) (Plummer 1896: 1.45, 90, 97, 138-39, 142, 159, 230, 243, 264).[4] So the -*a* in *Hreda* may be a Latin rather than an Old English inflexional ending.

hrēod 'reed'

An etymological connection between *Hreda* and OE *hrēod* does not seem at all likely. Bede appears to have represented Old English diphthongs by digraphs, usually the same digraphs employed in later Old English texts (Ström 1939: 98-101; Anderson 1941: 103-5; van Els 1972: 198-9; Shaw 2008). The diphthong /eːo/ most commonly appears in early manuscripts of Bede's writings as <eo>, for instance in the names *Ceolfrid*, *Ceolred* and *Ceolwulf* (van Els 1972: 79 and 199). Of particular relevance here is the month-name *weodmonað*, which appears in the manuscripts of *De Temporum Ratione* collated by Jones only in forms with digraphs (and occasionally trigraphs) representing the vowel sound in *weod-*: <eo> appears 13 times, while <eu> appears 12 times, with one each of the spellings <ea>, <aeo> and <aea> (Jones 1943: 211-13; Jones 1977: 330-1). The diphthong of *hrēod* developed from a diphthong in the common ancestor of Old English, Old Saxon and Old High German, as can be seen by the cognates of *hrēod* in these two languages: *hriod* and *hriot* (Holthausen 1954: under *hriod*; Kluge and Seebold 2002: under *Ried*[1]). We also possess a very early attestation of *hrēod* in the *Erfurt Glossary* in the spelling <hreod> (Pheifer 1974: 16). This spelling confirms that we should expect a diphthong in this word in early Old English, although of course the *Erfurt Glossary* does not reflect Bede's dialect:

nevertheless, we can be quite confident, given the examples from early Bede manuscripts quoted above, that a spelling *hred-* would be anomalous in Bede's dialect, and we might expect instead a spelling <hreod> or <hreud>. This is, in fact, very close to the attested spelling of the word *hreod* as a place-name element in the early manuscripts of Bede's *Historia Ecclesiastica*, where, as van Els (1972: 151) notes, the name *hreutford* occurs (van Els identifies this as Redbridge in Hampshire). Indeed, this word is remarkably consistently represented with a digraph throughout the Old English period, with just over a hundred attestations, of which around a hundred are in the form *hreod-* (*DOEC*). One instance of the form *hred-* appears in a charter, but *hreod-* forms are clearly the norm in such documents.[5] Even if Bede's representation of the name *Hreda* is conditioned by a written source from elsewhere in England, therefore, we would expect forms with digraphs. Moreover, the name *Hreda* appears in all the manuscripts of *De Temporum Ratione* collated by Jones with <e> as the sole vowel graph in the first syllable (Jones 1943: 211-12): although the consonants fluctuate slightly across these manuscripts, we never have <eo> or any other digraph instead of <e>. If her name were etymologically connected with *hrēod*, we might reasonably expect to see some evidence that the vowel sound in the first syllable of her name was a diphthong. We can therefore dismiss a connection with *hrēod* as unlikely.

hrēða 'goatskin'

The word *hrēða* is attested only three times in *DOEC*, all three instances occurring in the Latin-Old English glossaries in British Library, Cotton Cleopatra A.iii, usually known as the *Cleopatra Glossaries* (*DOEC* D8.1, 4005 and D8.3, 0562 and 0973). In these glossaries it glosses the Latin *melote*, which originally referred to a sheepskin worn as a garment (Lewis and Short: under *melota*). This word seems to have entered the gloss tradition as part of a group of *glossae collectae* gleaned from Aldhelm's *De Virginitate* (Kittlick 1998: 33-49). Bosworth-Toller glosses *hrēða* as 'a garment made of goat's skin' (under *hrēða*), but the Supplement adds the broader sense 'a mantle' (under *hrēða*). Clark Hall follows this lead, giving the gloss 'covering of goat-skin, mantle' (under *hrēða*). Whether *hrēða* ever implied a goatskin covering or garment is, however, uncertain. The Latin *melote* is glossed not only by *hrēða*, but also by *scrūd*, a much commoner word that clearly means 'clothing, covering' (Napier 1900: 97). Anglo-Saxon scholars no doubt knew Isidore's description of the *melote* in his *Etymologiae*, which does describe a cloak made of goatskin: 'Melotes, quae etiam pera vocatur, pellis est caprina [a] collo pendens praecincta usque ad lumbos' ('*Melotes*, which is also called *pera*, is the skin of a goat hanging from the neck and belted together down to the loins'; Lindsay 1911: book 19, chapter 24, section 19; my translation). This is, no doubt, the source of an Old English gloss translating *melotes* or *pera* as an over-garment of goatskin or (surprisingly but interestingly) badgerskin (*DOEC* D1.4, 0801). The fact that Anglo-Saxons knew that *melote* referred to a goatskin cloak does not, however, prove that they used *hrēða* as a gloss for this word because *hrēða* itself meant 'goatskin garment'. The fact that *scrūd* is also employed as a gloss for *melote* demonstrates the falsity of such a line of reasoning. Old English glosses of Latin words need not be exact equivalents for the words they gloss, but rather they give a possible meaning for the Latin word, which may be more or less exact. This meaning may well be conditioned by the context in which a glossator found a word in a Latin text, so that a Latin word with a range of meanings might be glossed in accordance with whichever of those meanings is most appropriate in the text the glossator was glossing. We are probably safer to suppose that *hrēða* refers to some sort of covering, without assuming that it has any more specific significance.

Bosworth-Toller connects *hrēða* with the terms *bordhrēoða* and *scildhrēoða*, which are both terms found mainly in poetry (under *hrēða*; see also Gradon 1977: 31). The former is glossed in its own entry in Bosworth-Toller as 'the cover or protection of the shield' and 'a shield, buckler', while *scildhrēoða* is glossed as 'shield-covering', 'a shield, buckler' and 'the arrangement of shields as in the *scild-burh*' (under *bordhrēoða* and *scildhrēoða*). These glosses are partly founded on an analysis of the second element of these compounds, *hrēoða*, as derived from a verb *hrēoðan*. Damico (1984: 76) suggests a form *hreodan*, but this would not satisfactorily account for the <ð> in *hrēoða*. The verb *hrēoðan* is attested only by its past participle (itself often used as part of compounds) *hroden*, which Bosworth-Toller glosses as 'laden, laden with ornaments, ornamented, adorned' (under *hroden*). In the entry for *bordhrēoða*, the verb *hrēoðan* is glossed 'to cover, protect' (under *bordhrēoða*). There are two implicit arguments here: first, that *hrēoðan has a general sense 'to cover', but is usually used with the narrower sense 'to adorn [by covering]', and that -hrēoða develops from the more general sense; secondly, that hrēða is in fact a use of -hrēoða as a simplex, although it is always attested outside glossaries as an element in the compounds bordhrēoða and scildhrēoða. The second of these arguments may have been prompted by the forms sceldreda and sceldhrēða, which appear in the Épinal and Erfurt glossaries respectively, in both cases glossing the Latin word testudo 'tortoise' (Pheifer 1974: 52). This Latin term was also employed to refer to the military formation in which Roman soldiers held their shields together above their heads to produce a continuous protective covering against missiles. This formation was briefly described by Isidore (Lindsay 1911: book 18, chapter 12, section 6), and it is clear that the compiler of the *Épinal-Erfurt Glossary* had some understanding of what was involved, as the alternative brodthaca (literally 'shield-thatch') also appears in this entry (Pheifer 1974: 52). As Pheifer (1974: 127) notes, brodthaca has the sense 'ceiling' rather than 'phalanx', but, as Isidore makes clear (Lindsay 1911: book 15, chapter 8, section 8), testudo is used in reference to a temple ceiling that is convex like a shield. It seems likely, therefore, that the *Épinal-Erfurt* compiler (who clearly knew Isidore's Etymologiae: see Pheifer 1974: xlv) used a compound containing the word bord 'board, shield' because of a knowledge of Isidore's likening of this type of ceiling to a shield.

The absence of forms of hrēða with <eo> spellings does present a problem if we wish to relate this word to bordhrēoða and scildhrēoða, but given that there are only three attestations of hrēða in the *Dictionary of Old English Corpus*, we cannot make a strong case against an identification of hrēða with -hrēoða. Since all three instances occur in the Cleopatra glossaries (*DOEC* D8.1, 4005 and D8.3, 0562 and 0973), they are unlikely to be independent of one another. There is also one case of bordhrēoða spelt with <e> rather than <eo>: in *Elene* the form bordhreðan (Gradon 1977: 31, line 122) occurs. It is, then, quite possible that -hrēoða had a variant form -hrēða, identical with the simplex hrēða, in some variety or varieties of Old English. On the other hand, it is not impossible that the very small number of cases of spellings with <e> rather than <eo> are due to scribal error. This presents some difficulties for an interpretation of Hreda as related to hrēða. If the usual form is, in fact, *hrēoða*, then we might raise the same objections as we did with Old English *hrēod*, that Old English /eːo/ usually appears in Bede's writings and in early Old English texts as a digraph, and we have no evidence for such a spelling of *Hreda*. Alternatively, we might accept either that *hrēða* is unrelated to *-hrēoða*, or that spellings with <e> rather than <eo> are a normal variant. In either case, we cannot rule out the possibility of a connection with *Hreda*; but there seem to be better grounds for seeing *hrēoða* as the regular form, and, therefore, as unconnected with *Hreda*.

hrēðe 'fierce'

The adjective *(h)rēðe* 'fierce' and its relatives appear much more often in *DOEC* in forms without initial <h> than with. The etymology of this word is somewhat problematic, although it is possible that it is related to Old High German *ruod* 'a roaring' (Pokorny 1959-69: 1.860). This leaves little scope for the use of cognates in other Germanic languages as evidence for its development. It is clear, however, that forms without <h> occur even in quite early Old English texts, for the *Corpus Glossary* (produced probably around the end of the eighth century, but drawing on glossarial traditions which are likely to stretch back as far as the late seventh century: see Herren 1998: 97-101) contains the glosses 'Ferox: roeðe' and 'Violenter: roeðelice' (Lindsay 1921: 76 and 183). It is quite likely, given the preponderance of forms with initial <r>, that this is, in fact, the original form, and that forms with initial <hr> are the result of analogical influence from words such as *hraðe*. This does not mean, however, that we should rule out a relationship between the name *Hreda* and *hrēðe*.

A more significant indication of non-relationship is provided by the presence in non-West Saxon texts of forms where the stem vowel is spelt <oe>. The *Corpus Glossary* forms noted above feature here, as do the forms *hroeðnise* in the *Durham Ritual* glosses and Lindisfarne Gospel glosses, *hroeðo/roeðo* in the Lindisfarne Gospel glosses, *roeðnis* in the Old English Bede, and *roeðe* in the Rushworth and Lindisfarne gospel glosses and in hymn 11 of the Vespasian Psalter (Lindelöf 1927: 122; Stevenson and Waring 1854-65: 1.13, 1.84, 3.24, 3.60; Miller 1890-98: 1.384, 1.386; Kuhn 1965: 158). These forms are the norm in the Lindisfarne, Rushworth and Durham glosses, which are all texts of Mercian or

Northumbrian origin (Hogg 1992: §§ 1.7-1.8), but forms with <e> are much more common in the Old English Bede (Miller 1890-98: 2.472 and 2.475, for instance, indicates that forms with <e> rather than <oe> appear in the places noted above in all manuscripts except T): this is consistent with the mixed Mercian/West-Saxon character of the text that generated considerable controversy in the first half of the twentieth century (Miller 1890-98: 1.xxvi-lix; Campbell 1951; Whitelock 1962: 57-8; Kuhn 1972). The <oe> spelling is characteristic of non-West Saxon varieties, where it usually represents the i-mutated form of /o(:)/. In West Saxon texts, this sound is generally represented by <e> (Campbell 1959: § 198). The implication of the <oe> spellings noted above, then, is that *hrēðe* derives from a prehistoric Old English form something like *(h)rōði*, and that the /i/ in the second syllable caused i-mutation of the /oː/ in the first.

In the earliest manuscripts of Bede's *Historia Ecclesiastica*, the i-mutation vowel derived from /o(:)/ is, as in other texts from Northumbria, regularly represented by the digraph <oi> or <oe> (Ström 1939: 97-8; Anderson 1941: 101-2; van Els 1972: 195-6). We would therefore expect a form <hroida> or <hroeda> rather than <hreda> in *De Temporum Ratione*, if the name *Hreda* were related to *hrēðe*. If Bede is repeating a form from a source from elsewhere in England, <oe> would be expected, with the possible exception of a West Saxon source, although even West Saxon may still have had the rounded vowel indicated by <oe> spellings at this early date (Hogg 1992: § 5.77). Again, none of the manuscripts collated by Jones include such a form (Jones 1943: 211-12), and on that basis we can conclude that it is unlikely that Hreda derives her name from the word *hrēðe*. This also disposes of Page's suggestion (1995: 126) that the month-name might derive directly from the word *hrēðe* rather than the name of a goddess.

hrēðan 'to rejoice'

This weak verb is attested only in the Old English poem *Exodus* (line 574): 'Hreðdon hildespelle, siððan hie þam herge wiðforon' ('they rejoiced with a battle-song, after they escaped from the army': Lucas 1977: 146; my translation). The verb is probably closely related to the more common (though still restricted to poetry) noun *hrēð* 'victory, glory', as they express related concepts. The discussion of *hrēð* below, therefore, can be taken to reflect the position for both *hrēð* and *hrēðan*.

hrēð 'victory, glory'

This word has been a favourite contender for the etymology of the name *Hreda*. Simek apparently has this in mind when he glosses Hreda (under the headword *Hrêðe*, which presumably represents his estimation of what the Old English version of her name would have been, had it been recorded) as ' "the famous", "the victorious"?' (1993: under *Hrêðe*). His explanation, however, simply refers to Grimm's attempt to relate the name to the Old Norse word *hróðr* 'fame' (Grimm 1882-88: 1.290).

As we have seen, Bede does use <d> to represent Old English /ð/, and there is therefore no reason why *Hreda* should not be related to *hrēð* on the basis of this consonant, and the initial consonant cluster is also formally identical. However, the Old Norse cognate *hróðr* has a different stem vowel, and this raises a significant problem for any interpretation of *Hreda* as related to *hrēð*. The o-vocalism of the Old Norse cognate is also present in the related Gothic adjective *hroþeigs*, and this suggests that the primitive Old English form probably also had an o-vocalism, which then developed into the e-vocalism which appears in the extant texts. Such a change could be caused by i-mutation, which, in the West Saxon dialect of Old English, produces /e:/ from /o:/. However, as noted above, this i-mutation produces <oi> or <oe> spellings in early manuscripts of Bede's work, and this therefore suggests that the name *Hreda* is unlikely to be related to *hrēð*. The situation is essentially the same as for *hrēðe* 'fierce'.

hræd/hræð/hreð 'quick'

The adjective *hræd* 'quick' generally appears with the stem vowel /æ/, but, like other adjectives with this stem vowel, it has a tendency for /ɑ/ to replace /æ/ as the stem vowel in some inflexional forms (see Campbell 1959: § 643). Forms with /e/ as the stem vowel, are, however, unusual outside the Mercian dialect, where the sound change known as Second Fronting causes /æ/ to be raised to /e/, particularly in West Mercian varieties (Hogg 1992: § 5.87). Thus the Vespasian Psalter glosses –

which are, as Kitson (2002: 478) remarks, 'notoriously west Mercian' – consistently have forms of the adjective *hræd*, and the related adverbs *hræðe* and *hrædlice*, with the stem vowel spelt <e> (Kuhn 1965: 4, 10, 32, 42, 64, 77, 96, 103, 140, 144). Forms of the adjective or the related adverbs with <e> for the stem vowel crop up occasionally elsewhere in the Old English corpus, but they are rare. This may bode ill for a possible relationship between *Hreda* and *hræd*. We would not expect Bede's dialect to show any sign of Second Fronting, yet the name *Hreda* always appears with the stem vowel graph <e> in the manuscripts of *De Temporum Ratione* collated by Jones.[6] In the earliest manuscripts of Bede's *Historia Ecclesiastica*, the Anglo-Saxon personal names and place-names recorded indicate that Bede usually represented /æ/ as <ae> or <ę> (van Els 1972: 182). We should therefore expect *Hreda* to be spelt <hraeda> or <hręda> if it is related to *hræd*, rather than with <e> representing the stem vowel.

There are, however, some other points we should consider. One is Bede's use of e-caudata <ę> to represent /æ(:)/. If *Hreda* was originally spelt <hręda>, as noted above, the recorded spellings with <e> could all derive from a misreading of <ę> as <e> very early in the manuscript transmission of *De Temporum Ratione*. Such a mistake would be relatively easy to make, and if it occurred before large numbers of copies of the text were in circulation, then it is possible that the erroneous reading might have been copied repeatedly, while the correct reading was lost with the small number of manuscripts that recorded it. Such a process could produce a situation in which the surviving manuscripts all record the erroneous <e> spelling.

The eighth-century manuscript fragments (Bückeburg, Niedersächsisches Staatsarchiv, dep. 3/1 fols i-viii; Landesarchiv Nordrhein-Westfalen Staatsarchiv Münster, Msc. I. 243, fols. 1r-2v, 11r-12v; Darmstadt, Hessische Landes- und Hochschulbibliothek, 4262) in Northumbrian uncial containing parts of *De Temporum Ratione* appear to have been subject, in Wallis's view, to 'heavy use and copying' (1999: lxxxvi). They do not include the relevant chapter, so we cannot be sure what their readings were, but their fragmentary state could be consistent with a model in which early manuscripts were lost, with the potential for losing the original reading for the name *Hreda*. Given the care and consistency with which the text appears to have been copied (Jones

1943: 140; Wallis 1999: lxxxvii), however, and the quite large number of manuscripts of ninth-century date, it seems on the whole more likely than not that an original reading <hręda> would have been preserved in at least some of the ninth-century manuscripts.

The other issue we should consider is the possibility of another sound change affecting Bede's spelling of *Hreda*. In early manuscripts of the *Historia Ecclesiastica*, the i-mutated form of /æ/ appears as <e>, for instance in the personal names *Ecgberct*, *Ecgfrid*, *Herebald* and *Hereric* (van Els 1972: 186; see Campbell 1959: §§ 575-7 and §§ 590-2 for details of the development of the nouns *ecg* and *here*). We could, therefore, posit that *Hreda* was developed from *hræd* as a feminine noun with *i/j* forming the end of the stem (as is the case with *ecg*: see Campbell 1959: § 591). However, nouns such as *ecg* typically show doubling of the final consonant of the stem, which is not present in *Hreda*. If *Hreda* develops along the pattern of this sort of noun, therefore, it does not behave in exactly the same way as an ordinary noun would.

There is the possibility, then, that if Bede received his month-names from a Mercian source, *Hreda* could be related to *hræd*. There are some indications that a more southerly source should be sought, however, which suggests that we should be cautious in advancing *hræd* as an etymological relative for *Hreda*. Nevertheless, since *hræd* is more plausible than the other potential relatives identified above, we should keep it in mind, despite the difficulties that remain with such an interpretation.

Later forms of the month-name

The month-name *Hredmonað* is not unique to *De Temporum Ratione*, but also appears in a number of later Anglo-Saxon texts. Comparison of the forms used in these texts against that used in *De Temporum Ratione* provides us with a way of double-checking our etymological reasoning. If, for instance, we were to discover later forms such as **hroedmonað* then we might wish to reconsider the possibility of a relationship with *hrēð* 'victory' or *hrēðe* 'fierce'.

Where then, do we find later instances of *Hredmonað*? Table 5 outlines the texts and forms known to the present author.

Manuscript	Form	Edition
Oxford, Bodleian Library, Ashmole 328 (S.C. 6882, 7420) [Byrhtferth's *Enchiridion*]	*Hreðmonð*	Baker and Lapidge 1995: 24
Cambridge, Trinity College, R.15.32 (945) [calendar]	*Hrêod monað*	Wormald 1934: 130
Oxford, Bodleian Library, Douce 296 (S.C. 21870) [calendar]	*HRÆDMONAÞ*	Wormald 1934: 256
Cambridge, Corpus Christi College, 422 [calendar]	*Hrædd*	Wormald 1934: 186 (appears in *DOEC* as C88)
London, British Library, Cotton Vitellius E.xviii [calendar]	*Hræd monað*	Wormald 1934: 158
Rouen, Bibliothèque municipale, Y.6 (274) [Missal of Robert of Jumièges]	*hredmonað*	Wilson 1896: 11
Oxford, St John's College, 17 [notes from Bede]	*Reðmonð*	Baker and Lapidge 1995: 396
London, British Library, Cotton Julius A.x [Old English Martyrology]	*Hredmonað*	Kotzor 1981: 2.27
London, British Library, Cotton Julius A.x Cambridge, Corpus Christi College, 196 [Old English Martyrology]	*Hreðmonað*	Kotzor 1981: 2.48

Table 5. Post-Bedan forms of *Hredmonað*.

Apart from the single instance of *Hrêod monað*, spellings with <e> and <æ> are the norm. This could be seen as strengthening the case for an etymological relationship with *hræd* 'quick'. This also reinforces the case against the other possible relatives discussed above. The fluctuation between <e> and <æ> spellings, however, remains puzzling. The possibility of a specifically Mercian form with <e>, as opposed to <æ> in other dialects, was raised above, but while there is nothing in the data assembled above to disprove such patterning, neither is there sufficient data to prove it. Of course, one might argue that the <e> spellings represent transmission of Bede's spelling, rather than the author's own spelling, but in any case this does not explain the presence of <æ> spellings. The reason for the variation between <e> and <æ> spellings of the name must therefore be sought elsewhere.

Hreda and the onomasticon

Having examined the various words which might be etymologically related to the name *Hreda*, we can discount some, such as *hrēod*, as highly unlikely, and we have also seen that several that look, on first glance, more promising, are quite unlikely. The words *hrēðe* 'fierce', *hrēoða* 'covering', and *hrēð* 'victory, glory' all present considerable problems. The evidence is perhaps not so copious, nor sufficiently straightforward, to allow us to discount these options entirely, but special pleading is required if we are accept one of these as etymologically related to the name *Hreda*. Given the stability of the text of *De Temporum Ratione* in its ninth-century manuscripts (Jones 1943: 140), we may be reasonably confident that scribal error would not have obscured completely an etymological link with one of our rejected options. Since we have a reasonable body of independent evidence for Bede's own Old English orthography in the earliest manuscripts of the *Historia Ecclesiastica*, moreover, we have been able to check our possible relatives against this evidence, and have found that they do not fit with it. The evidence of later forms of the month-name also tends to confirm our rejection of these options. We are left with a relationship with *hræd* 'quick', and the later forms of the month-name are consonant with this interpretation. We might, therefore, tentatively suggest that Hreda's name relates her in some way to the idea of speed.

This is not the end of our search, however, for we have not yet considered possible relationships with other names (both personal and tribal) attested in Old English sources. Our experience with Eostre suggests that we should at least consider the possibility of a relationship with toponymy or group-names, and perhaps also with personal names. The Old English personal name *Hrethhun*, borne by a ninth-century Bishop of Leicester, appears to be formed with the element *hrēð* (*PASE*: under *Hrethhun 1*; *Ræthhun 1* appears to be the same individual, and *Ræthhun 2*, a ninth-century Abbot of Abingdon, could also be the same man, judging by the dates of attestation of the two). The element *hrēð* is also compounded with *gota* ('Goth') to produce a term *Hrēðgotan*, which refers to the Goths, in two Old English poems, and in each case the term is used as a simplex as well. These names may, then, help to shed further light on *Hreda*.

Hrēð as a personal name element

The sequence <hrēð> occurs as a prototheme in a number of Old English personal names. In some cases, it may be an i-mutated form of the more common <hroð>. This is evident in the form <hroethberht[e]> that appears on an inscribed stone from Falstone, Northumberland (Okasha 1971: no. 39; Cramp 1984: 1.172, vol. 2 plate 166; Okasha 2004: 96). Anglo-Saxon *libri vitae* also include several of instances with the characteristic non-West Saxon <oe> spelling: Gerchow's index of this material notes the forms *Hroeðberct, Hroeðburg, Hroeðgeoful Hroeðgifu, Hroeðlac, Hroeðwald* and *Hroeðuini* (Gerchow 1988: 394). However, the name *Hrethhun* seems to be an exception, appearing in a variety of spellings with <e> and <æ> as the vowel of the prototheme (*PASE*: under *Hrethhun 1, Ræthhun 1* and *Ræthhun 2*). The spellings with <æ> could suggest parallels with Frankish name forms such as *Chradobercthus* (Kölzer, Hartmann and Stieldorf 2001: 1.219), and we should also consider the name of Hreðel, the father of the Geatish king Hygelac in *Beowulf*. Like *Hrethhun*, *Hreðel* appears with both <e> and <æ> spellings. Fulk (1992: 317) seeks to explain the <æ> spellings as the result of 'archaic and/or Northumbrian *æ*' being misread by a scribe, on the assumption that *Hreðel* must contain the element *hröð* in its i-mutated form (the *-el* suffix derives from an original **-ila-* suffix that usually causes i-mutation of the vowel of the root element; see Peterson 2004: 39 and 50, and compare the individuals in *PASE* called *Putta* with *Pyttel 1*). Given that the name *Hrethhun* appears with both <e> and <æ> spellings, but never <oe> spellings, it is simpler to suppose that *Hreðel* and *Hrethhun* are formed on a different root from *hröð*. This root shows an alternation between e-vocalisms and æ-vocalisms which could represent the same sort of variation between i-mutated and unmutated forms seen in the name element *hröð/hreð* (related to the Old English word *hreð* 'victory, glory', discussed above) and in Old English names such as *Hædde* (*PASE*: under *Hædde 1-3*). If this is indeed a case of forms with and without i-mutation, then the vowel of this name element must be short, as i-mutation affects only short /æ/ (Campbell 1959: § 191). This would therefore suggest that the name element derives from *hræð* 'quick', the only word discussed above with a short stem vowel. This would fit with the evidence of continental Germanic names such as *Chradobercthus*, which clearly demonstrate the existence of a prototheme *chrad* 'swift' beside the commoner *chrod* 'fierce' (for the latter, see Reichert 1987-90: 2.549-50).

The Merovingian names in *Chrad-*, however, are not the only possible parallel for an Old English name element spelt <hræd> or <hræð>.

Old Norse runic inscriptions provide evidence for an Old Norse name element (alongside *hróðr* and *hraðr*, related to Old English *Hroð* and *hræd*, respectively) *hreið* (**hraiþ** in early runic inscriptions; see Peterson 2007: under *Hróð-*, *Hraði*, *Hræið-*). This should correspond to an Old English **hrāð* or **hrād*, but **hræð* or **hræd* could be produced by i-mutation. Forms with the stem vowel spelt <e> should not occur in most varieties of Old English, but, as we shall see (p. 91), some early Kentish and Mercian texts do contain such spellings. It is difficult, therefore, to decide whether the name *Hrethhun*, which appears in both <e> and <æ> spellings, has the element *hræð* or a putative **hrǣð*, related to the Old Norse name element: both are possible.

The personal names and the month-name evidence seem, then, to suggest two possible relatives for *Hreda*. One is the adjective *hræð* 'quick', which also appears as a name element. The variation between the stem vowels /e/ and /æ/ in the case of this element can be explained not in terms of dialect difference, but in terms of a common alternation between i-mutated and unmutated forms in personal name elements. On the other hand, we also have the possibility of a name element **hrǣð*, related to the Old Norse personal name element *hreið-*. The etymological origins of this name element are uncertain. It is difficult, however, to decide which of these elements is involved, since they are liable to be spelt in the same way in Old English. Nevertheless, like Eostre, Hreda appears to have a name that derives from a word that is also used as a personal name element. Moreover, in both cases the name element is not a common one in Anglo-Saxon England, as far as we can tell from the surviving records. Possibly these name elements began to fall out of use during the Anglo-Saxon period, although the reasons for such a decline are not easy to determine: while *ēastor* may have suffered from the application of the term to one of the major Christian festivals, *hræd* or **hrǣð* are not obviously problematic, and the adjective *hræd* – to which the former name element would seem to be transparently related – continued in use through the Old English period and into Middle English (although its meaning changed somewhat in Middle English). Another possibility is that these name elements became less popular because of their connection with pre-Christian deities, but this does not seem entirely likely, given that other name elements that relate to pre-Christian religious life, such as *ōs*, continued to be common. We may simply be dealing with the vagaries of name-giving fashions. If we are to seek an explanation in the connotations or associations of a name-element, we may find a more plausible one in the relationship between these name elements and group-names. In any case, the relationship between *Eostre* and the personal-name element *ēastor* can also be seen as part of a relationship between the name of the deity and names applied in naming socio-politically defined groups or areas. A similar connection between deity and socio-political group can also be posited for Hreda.

The *Hreðgotan*

Hreðgotan is a name applied to the Goths (usually *Gotan* in Old English) in two Old English poems: *Widsith* and *Elene*. The first is a short poem preserved in a single copy in the manuscript known as the Exeter Book (Exeter, Library of the Dean and Chapter of Exeter Cathedral, 3501), a large and miscellaneous collection of Old English poems, written in the later tenth century, perhaps at Crediton or Exeter, and very probably left to the community at Exeter by Bishop Leofric on his death in 1072 (Muir 1994: 1.1-3). The other poem is much longer, and is the second longest poem in the Vercelli Book (Vercelli, Biblioteca Capitolare, CXVII), an Anglo-Saxon manuscript containing a small number of Old English poems that appears to have been in Vercelli in Italy within around a century and a half of its production in the later tenth century (Krapp 1932: xvii-xx; Scragg 1992: xxiii-xxv).

Widsith presents a brief account, consisting mainly of lists of tribes and their kings, of the travels of the poet whose name provides the modern title of the poem. Widsith's wanderings would have involved a lifespan of hundreds of years, and his name, which literally means 'wide journey' – or, as Muir (1994: 2.520) renders it, 'he who journeys widely' – seems to suggest that the central purpose of the poem is its cataloguing of tribes and kings, rather than to trace the life-story of Widsith himself. The poem is, essentially, about issues of tradition and rulership, rather than the narrator as an individual. We might be tempted to identify this poem as an Anglo-Saxon gesture towards an idea of a pan-Germanic ethnicity, but, while Anglo-Saxons were capable of recognising relationships with other Germanic groups (as, for instance, in the treatment of the continental Saxons by Bede and Boniface: see Plummer 1896: 1.296;

Colgrave and Mynors 1969: 476-7; Tangl 1916: no. 46), pan-Germanism is a rather more modern mindset. The groups catalogued in *Widsith* include not just Germanic tribes, but also the Greeks, the Romans, the Finns, the Scots, the Picts and even the Saracens, Israelites, Assyrians, Persians and Indians. Most of these groups are dealt with in fairly cursory fashion, but the Goths are not; and in fact the poem mentions this group in particular on several occasions, with a particular focus on the Gothic king Eormenric at lines 5-9, 88-92 and in the following passage:

> Ðonan ic ealne geondhwearf   eþel Gotena,
> sohte ic a gesiþa   þa selestan –
> þæt wæs innweorud   Earmanrices.
> Hehcan sohte ic ond Beadecan   ond Herelingas;
> Emercan sohte ic ond Fridlan   ond Eastgotan,
> frodne ond godne   fæder Unwenes;
> Seccan sohte ic ond Beccan,   Seafolan ond Þeodric,
> Heaþoric ond Sifecan,   Hliþe ond Incgenþeow;
> Eadwine sohte ic ond Elsan,   Ægelmund ond Hungar,
> ond þa wloncan gedryht   Wiþmyrginga;
> Wulfhere sohte ic ond Wyrmhere –   ful oft þær wig ne alæg,
> þonne Hræda here   heardum sweordum
> ymb Wistlawudu   wergan sceoldon
> ealdne eþelstol   Ætlan leodum (Muir 1994: 1.245, lines 109-22)

From there I travelled throughout the whole land of the Goths. I constantly visited the best of comrades, who were the company of Eormanric's household. I visited Hethca and Beadeca and the Herelingas. I visited Emerca and Fridla and Eastgota the wise and good, father of Unwen. I visited Secca and Becca, Seafola and Theodric, Heathoric and Sifeca, Hlithe and Incgentheow. I visited Eadwine and Elsa, Ægelmund and Hungar and the high-mettled nation of the Withmyrgingas. I visited Wulfhere and Wyrmhere; not very often was there respite from warfare there, when the army of the Goths with tough swords had to defend their ancestral seat near the Vistula Forest against the people of Attila. (Bradley 1997: 340)

5. Hreda

In this passage, the Goths are referred to by the simplex *Hræda*, but at line 57 the compound *Hreðgotum* appears. In line 7 Eormenric is termed a *hreðcyning* ('*hreð*-king'), a unique attestation of this compound, which can probably be considered a derivative of the element *Hreð-*. Etymological analysis of *Hræd-/Hreð-* is complicated by the possibility that Old English speakers identified this name element with the word *hrēð* 'victory, glory', discussed above (Smith 1931: 331). Parallels with Scandinavian traditions, moreover, suggest that *Hræd-/Hreð-* may have been borrowed from Old Norse (Anderson 1999: 41-3) – a process of transmission that could conceivably obscure etymological links. We will return to these Scandinavian traditions shortly, but we should also briefly outline the role of the Goths in *Elene* before doing so.

Elene is in some ways a quite different sort of poem from *Widsith*. While *Widsith* is brief and allusive, with only gestures towards a narrative, *Elene* is a lengthy narrative poem recounting the adventures of the empress Helen, mother of Constantine the Great, in her search for the True Cross. It opens (giving a date of 233, around a hundred years too early for the events depicted) with Constantine on the brink of battle with the *Hreðgotan*, Huns, Franks, and probably (though the manuscript reading is *hunas*) with the Hugas (Gradon 1977: 26 lines 20-1; Bradley 1997: 166). Constantine receives a vision of the Cross prior to the battle, and orders a standard to be made in this form: the result is victory (Gradon 1977: 29-33; Bradley 1997: 167-9). The vision of the Cross is, of course, strikingly similar to earlier accounts of the battle of the Milvian Bridge; but the army of *Hreðgotan*, Huns, Franks and Hugas, whom Constantine defeats on the shores of the Danube, clearly do not tally with the forces of Maxentius, defeated in Italy. The overall impression is of a tradition in which various elements of Constantine's reign have been conflated: the battle of the Milvian Bridge has perhaps been confused with campaigns against Licinius, who employed Gothic mercenaries, and perhaps also with the campaign of Constantine's son, Constantine II, against the Goths around the Danube in 332 AD (Wolfram 1990: 61). The latter campaigns were directed against the Visigoths under Ariaric, rather than the Ostrogoths of Ermanaric, which may suggest that Old English *Hreðgotan* was not simply a designation for one of the two major Gothic groupings. Smith (1931: 331) argues plausibly that the term was used indiscriminately in Old English to refer to Goths of whatever affiliation.

89

Nevertheless, *Widsith* and *Elene* are consonant in using the term *Hreðgotan* in referring to fourth-century Goths, during a period when they were settled around the northern borders of the eastern Roman Empire. In this respect they seem to reflect a particular concern of later sources with the Gothic rulers of this period, among whom Ermanaric was perhaps the best known and most often depicted in medieval texts. The Old English textual traditions are, however, rather thin on details of the *Hreðgotan*, and we should therefore consider the evidence for this group in Scandinavian sources. It has long been noted that the Old English *Hreðgotan* have a very similar name to the *Reiðgotar* who appear in stanza 12 of the Eddaic poem *Vafþrúðnismál* (Machan 2008: 60). The alliterative metre of the line concerned requires a form *Hreiðgotar*, and, as we shall see, earlier evidence confirms that this was the original form (Machan 2008: 80). The name also appears in the territorial designation *Reiðgotaland*, which occurs in a number of Old Norse sagas (Jónsson 1950: 1.291, 1.299, 1.342, 1.344, 1.350, 2.27-9, 2.67, 2.82, 4.289). The earliest Scandinavian attestation of this group name appears on the Rök stone:

þat sakum ąnart huaʀ fur niu altum ąn urþi fiaru miʀ hraiþkutum auk tu miʀ ąn ubs (s)akaʀ raiþ (þ)iaurikʀ hin þurmuþi stiliʀ flutna strąntu hraiþmaraʀ sitiʀ nu karuʀ ą kuta sinum skialti ub fatlaþʀ skati mari(n)ka. (Gordon and Taylor 1957: 188)

This secondly let us tell, who, nine generations ago, was born among the Hreið-Goths, and afterwards perished among them through his overweening pride: Theoderic the brave of heart, lord of sea-rovers, ruled the strand of the Gothic sea (the Adriatic). Now he sits ready on his Gothic steed, a shield hung round his neck, the lord of the Mærings. (Gordon and Taylor 1957: 190)

This Viking Age memorial inscription from Rök in Östergötland, Sweden, seems to indicate the existence of parallel traditions across England and Scandinavia in relation to Theoderic, who is also connected with the Mærings in the Old English poem *Deor* (Wessén 1958: 76-7; Muir 1994: 1.284; Bradley 1997: 364). The inscription also provides important evidence for the etymology of the Old Norse group-name. *Hreiðgotar* clearly derives from a form with Proto-Germanic */ai/ for the stem vowel of *Hreið-*, appearing in the form **hraiþkutum** on the Rök inscription. Numerous scholars have noted that the Old English *Hreð-* cannot derive from such a form (see Chambers 1912: 252-3): Proto-Germanic */ai/ generally produces /ɑː/ in Old English (compare, for instance, Gothic *hailags* and Old English *hālig* 'holy'; Old Norse *bein* and Old English *bān* 'bone'). However, the form *Hræda* in *Widsith* could derive from Proto-Germanic */ai/ if it were affected by i-mutation. Thus Old English *hǣð* 'heath, wasteland' corresponds to Gothic *haiþi* (Bosworth-Toller: under *hǣþ*; Wright 1924: 326; Feist 1939: under *haiþi*; Krause 1968: 296). This led Chambers (1912: 253) to argue that Old English forms such as *Hreðgota* are the result of a 'false analogy' by which the vowel of *hrǣð-* was altered to match that of *hrēð* 'glory' (Machan 2008: 80 also notes the possibility of similar processes affecting the Old Norse name, but this might account for the replacement of *hreið-* by *reið-*, rather than affecting the vowel). This argument that folk-etymology has caused alteration of the vowel allows a case to be made for Old Norse *hreið-* and Old English *hrǣð-* as cognates – and moreover, if they are cognates, then they appear to be formally identical with the Old Norse personal name element *hreið-*.

It is not clear, however, that Bede's form <hreda> can be identified as containing the i-mutated form of Proto-Germanic */ai/. The evidence of the early manuscripts of Bede's *Historia Ecclesiastica* points quite clearly to his preference for <ae> as the spelling for this sound (van Els 1972: 197; Anderson 1941: 103). Nevertheless, we have noted in relation to *Eostre* that Bede appears to have been using – and preserving the spellings of – a source that did not use his own normal orthography. As Toon (1983: 166-9) has demonstrated, records of the Kentish variety of Old English from the early ninth century onwards often spell the i-mutated form of Proto-Germanic */ai/ as <e>. There is a lack of evidence for the situation prior to this in Kentish, but clearly we cannot rule out the possibility that a Kentish document available to Bede in the early eighth century would have included spellings of this sound as <e> rather than <ae>. Some Mercian sources also show signs of raising of this sound to /eː/ before dental consonants (Hogg 1992: § 5.79 note 1). There are, it would seem, dialects in which the spelling evidenced in the early manuscripts of *De Temporum Ratione* could be consistent with a connection of the name *Hreda* with Old Norse *hreið-* and Old English *hrǣð-*.

There is, then, the possibility that the name *Hreda* is etymologically connected with an element used in forming personal and group names, just as *Eostre* is. If this is the case, it is connected with an element of obscure meaning and origins. On the other hand, it is equally possible that *Hreda* is to be connected with the adjective *hræð* 'quick' and/or the related personal name element. The name *Hreda* clearly presents greater difficulties than *Eostre* in arriving at a single, clear conclusion – and it is unlikely that it will ever be possible to decide certainly between them. Nevertheless, we have managed to address some of the problems involved, and we have shown that Grimm's etymology is unlikely. And this returns us to a central issue in our examination of pre-Christian goddesses: Grimm's interpretation of Hreda was connected to the idea that she should have a function (in her case, perhaps a function associated with glory). As we have seen in the case of the Germanic matrons, and in the case of Eostre, the idea of function may not map well onto the religious experience of early Germanic groups. We have suggested above that Eostre is probably a deity associated with a specific group or area, and the fact that Hreda can plausibly be connected with a personal name element – and perhaps with a personal name element that also appears as part of a group name – indicates that her cult may well have been similarly defined.

If Hreda were bound up with group identity, however, the problem of the group involved remains. One would not necessarily expect Anglo-Saxons to name one of their months from a goddess associated with the Goths. Yet Anglo-Saxon personal names often involve an element related to a group-name. Some, such as *Seax-*, relate to obviously local groups (in this case, the Saxons), while others, such as *Swæf-* (Suebian) and *-gēat* (related to the southern Swedish people who appear in *Beowulf* as *Geatas*; see Jack 1994: 8), appear to relate to distant tribes. Of course, this might partly be explicable in terms of the heterogeneity of Anglo-Saxon settlement: the place-name *Swaffham* (*swǣfa-hām* 'settlement of the Suebi'), for instance, suggests that Suebi may have formed part of the mix in East Anglia (Ekwall 1960: under *Swaffham*; Mills 2003: under *Swaffham*; Cameron 1969: 72). However, it does not seem entirely satisfactory to suppose that such naming patterns are simply the result of a tribal melting pot. Name elements related to the names of distant tribes are not unusual elsewhere in Germania: thus we have, for instance, the name *swabaharjaz* on a rune-stone from Rö in Bohuslän, Sweden (Antonsen 1975: 43; Peterson 1994: 153-4), containing an element related to the name of the Suebi, and the name *Saxi* (variously spelt *sagsi, sahsi, sakse, saksi*, and probably related to the ethnic designation of the Saxons) on a number of Scandinavian rune-stones (Peterson 2007: under *Saxi*). This suggests that the interplay between group and personal naming practices is, in fact, a complex one, in which there is no simple correlation between the naming of individuals and their group affiliations (see also Peterson 1994: 154). Peterson (1994: 153-4) suggests possible ways of understanding name elements related to ethnic designations in terms of deliberate reference to ethnic groups, and notes the need for more work on such name elements. In doing this work, we should perhaps also consider the possibility that many of these name elements are in fact elements that existed at a very early stage in the Germanic dialects, encoding cultural values that were applicable both to the individual and to ethnic groups. Such name elements may not originally have been used with any intention of indexing particular ethnic groups.

The goddess Hreda clearly presents greater difficulties of interpretation than Eostre, but we can at least see that her name suggests similar interrelationships between personal and group naming practices and the naming of deities. As with Eostre, it seems reasonable to suppose that Hreda was in some way associated with a specific local grouping, although we can recover little of the nature of this association or the group involved. It is possible that Hreda herself was in some way conceived of as 'quick' (if we accept *hræð* as the etymology), but it is at least as possible that her name expresses her connection to an individual with this element in their name. The example of the Rodings in Essex, discussed in the previous chapter (see p. 68), perhaps indicates how individuals gave their names to territories and groups – and they may in the process also have given their names to goddesses. The example of the *matronae Arvagastiae*, whose name clearly relates to the Germanic personal name *Arvagast* (Derks 1998: 123), suggests a similar process of development from an individual, and we also considered above (p. 40) the case of the goddess-name *Vagdavercustis* and its relationship to the male personal name *Vagdavercustus*. On the other hand, we also have the possibility of an etymology from another personal name element that appears in Old

Norse as *hreið*, and which can also relate to a tribal grouping, although the etymology of the element itself remains uncertain (De Vries 1977: under *Hreiðgotar*; Peterson 2007: under *Hræið-*).

Transmission of *Hredmonað*

As with Eostre, this exploration of the goddess also raises questions about the month-name derived from her name. If *hredmonað* was initially specific to a particular area, then we might ask whether it spread across other areas of Anglo-Saxon England. While *eastermonað* evidently became associated with the Christian festival of Easter early on, and may thus have been disseminated in association with the festival, *hredmonað* does not possess this advantage. The extant attestations of *hredmonað* listed above (see Table 5, p. 83) suggest that this month-name may well have been largely the preserve of calendars and computistical materials in late Anglo-Saxon England – and this could very well be the result of the influence of *De Temporum Ratione* on such texts. We are lacking, in other words, clear evidence that *hredmonað* ever did achieve wide currency in Anglo-Saxon England. And there is, moreover, evidence that it was not the only native month-name that could be used for March. Ælfric uses the form *hlydan monðe* in his *De Temporibus Anni* (Henel 1942: 36), and also in his homily for Circumcisio Domini in the first series of his *Catholic Homilies*, where he claims that 'Se eahtateoða dæg þæs monðes þe we hatað martius þone ge hatað hlyda wæs se forma dæg þyssere worulde' ('the eighteenth day of the month that we call March, which you call Hlyda, was the first day of this world'; Clemoes 1997: 229; my translation). Forms of *hlyda* or *hlydanmonað* appear in a number of versions of a note on the three key Fridays of the year on which one should fast (Napier 1889: 3; Roeder 1904: xii; Henel 1934: 64-5). They also feature in a brief text (known in a number of manuscript versions) which details the days in each month when medical procedures should not be carried out, and claims that *hlyda* is the month in which the creation of the world took place, though without specifying a precise date as Ælfric does (Förster 1929: 266-9; Henel 1935: 336-7). This month-name continued in use in Middle English, where it appears in texts from southwestern England (*MED*: under *lide*). This pattern of attestation suggests that *hlydanmonað* was a southwestern dialect form, and provides an indication that native Old English month-names may well originally have been quite various and specific to particular areas, although little of this diversity survived into late Old English.

The diversity of native Germanic month-names on the Continent also suggests that Old English may well have started out with much more variety than we can discern in the extant corpus of Old English. One name attested on the Continent, moreover, is particularly important to our understanding of *hredmonað*: the existence of a month name *redmanot* in a small number of late medieval and early modern German sources formed part of Grimm's case for a goddess Hruoda/Hrede worshipped in England and on the Continent (Grimm 1882-88: 1.289-90). This argument was criticised by Weinhold on the basis that he believed Bede's goddess Hreda, like Eostre, to be an invention: he preferred to see the German *redmanot* and Old English *hreðmonað* as deriving from the related Old High German *hradi/redi* and Old English *hrað/hreð* 'quick' (Weinhold 1869: 53). More recently, Jeske has cited Weinhold's etymology as one possibility, though without indicating what weight he attaches to the claim (Jeske 1983: 38). Neither, however, explores the use of *hræð* as a personal name element, and it is clear that the existence of a continental *redmanot* raises questions about the relationship between Anglo-Saxon and continental Germanic month-names.

The evidence for *redmanot* on the Continent is, according to Jeske, largely restricted to Alemannic sources, although there are a few instances from elsewhere (1983: 38). This pattern could be seen as similar to the dialectal distribution of Old High German *ôstarun* (Frings and Müller 1966-68: 1.38 and map 6). We might, then, argue that *redmanot* represents a borrowing from Old English in the same context as the borrowing of Old English *ēastre* discussed above (see pp. 54 and 69). The evidence of Einhard's *Vita Karoli Magni* ('Life of Charlemagne'), however, suggests that *ôstarun* had more impact outside its initial area of adoption. In chapter 29, Einhard notes that Charlemagne sought to standardise the month-names in use among the Franks, and that the standardised names for March and April were *Lentzinmanoth* ('lenten month') and *Ostarmanoth* ('easter month') (Holder-Egger 1911: 33). The influence of the Bedan month-naming tradition, perhaps via Alcuin, has been suspected behind Charlemagne's *Ostarmanoth* (Hammer 1997: 12), but the adoption of *ôstarun* as a term for Easter (which evidently took place quite early; see Green 2000: 351) should also be considered as a potential context for Charlemagne's creation of the month-name *Ostarmanoth*. On the other hand, *redmanot*, whether it is related to Old English *hredmonað* or not, did not enjoy the same obvious connection to a Christian festival, and it is not entirely surprising, therefore, that Charlemagne did not employ this name, preferring to use or create names related to seasonal and agricultural cycles, except where a name might be related to a major Christian festival.

Conclusion

Hreda presents greater difficulties than Eostre, and there are at least two plausible etymologies for her name. It is noteworthy, however, that these etymologies both relate to terms used in forming personal names, and in one case to a term employed in group naming as well as personal naming. If Hreda's name is indeed related to a term employed as an ethnic designation, she, along with Eostre, can be seen as part of a broader pattern of deities and ancestor figures whose names connect with social groupings. Such figures are, not surprisingly, most obvious when they relate to well-known, often large-scale groupings: for instance, the deity Saxnot (whose name means 'companion of the Saxons', and who also crops up in a genealogy of the kings of Essex in the form *Seaxnet*; Gallée 1894: 245, Sweet 1885: 179) or the royal ancestor Gapt in Jordanes' *De Origine Actibusque Getarum* ('On the Origin and Deeds of the Goths'; Mommsen 1882: 76). Eostre, like the goddesses and matrons of the Romano-Germanic votive inscriptions, suggests the existence of many more such deities, operating at smaller social scales – and perhaps success stories like Saxnot and Gapt simply represent the result of snowballing of such figures when attached to small social groups which themselves become larger and more successful. We might, indeed, legitimately ask whether even some of the great gods could have developed along these lines.

Hreda, as ever, is an awkward case. While we might see her as deriving her name from some function related to notions of speed, the patterns noted above suggest that we should at least take seriously the possibility that her name draws on personal or group naming. We might see her as simply relating to a personal name element, perhaps implying that she was originally connected with a family who used that element in forming their own names. This would be consonant with some of the Romano-Germanic evidence that suggests overlap between human and divine name elements (see pp. 39-40). We could even place Eostre in the same context, although the geographical interpretation may seem somewhat likelier, in view of the apparent rarity of *ēastor* as a personal name element in Anglo-Saxon England. The possible connections between *Hreda* and a name applied to the Goths in Old English and Old Norse, however, suggest another possibility: *Hreda* could relate to a group name. That the group name in question is usually applied to the Goths is clearly troubling, but it is a name that appears to have formed part of English and Scandinavian traditions of the Goths. It is at least possible that this name element was employed in forming personal and/or group names closer to home, as well as becoming attached to narratives about the Goths.

6

Conclusion
Roles of the Northern Goddess?

In 1998 Hilda Ellis Davidson published a book entitled *Roles of the Northern Goddess*. The unspoken implication of its title is that there was a northern goddess, that the various goddesses Davidson discusses were in some way parts of a whole. The message of this book is, above all else, that we should be wary of such ideas of pan-Germanism or pan-northernism. The goddesses discussed in this book seem to point in the other direction, towards the tribal, the local, perhaps even the familial or personal. They represent, in all probability, the tip of an iceberg of irrecoverable deities who related in specific and contextually significant ways to their worshippers within a locality or socio-political grouping. This contrasts with models of pan-Germanic cults of the great gods, and although we cannot rule out the possibility that both local and pan-Germanic cults co-existed, the evidence presented here should at least prompt us to look carefully at the true extent and nature of the evidence for all Germanic deities, including the great gods. This is not, however, to reject any notion of common religious patterns across time and space in the Germanic-speaking world. On the contrary, we have seen that common patterns of name-giving, that run across the names of humans and their deities, form links – links that are in some ways part of the broader linguistic interconnections between the Germanic languages – between deities worshipped by very different Germanic groups in very different contexts.

We should also bear in mind the delicate balancing acts required in reading our textual sources for pre-Christian religion. As we have seen, understanding the goddesses mentioned in Bede's *De Temporum Ratione* requires not only a careful analysis of linguistic evidence, but also consideration of the complexities of a Christian author's conception of the pre-Christian past. Bede was undoubtedly sincere in his vote of thanks at the end of chapter 15 of *De Temporum Ratione* – 'Good Jesu, thanks be to thee, who hast turned us away from these vanities and given us [grace] to offer to thee the sacrifice of praise' (Wallis 1999: 54) – but this does not mean that he was necessarily interested in suppressing all memory of the pre-Christian past. Indeed, the sentiment here is clearly one that values the knowledge of previous benightedness as an earnest of the power of God's grace. The complexities of this attitude to Anglo-Saxon paganism were not, it seems to me, idiosyncratic, but part of a strong current within Christian Anglo-Saxon intellectual life that valued pre-Christian tradition as well as – perhaps even as part of – the propagation of Christianity.

Such points of contact between Christian intellectual culture and the pre-Christian past are, however, decidedly sparse, and the Christian authors of the Middle Ages were, as we know, decidedly prone to repetition of earlier authors' statements. What Bede and authors like him tell us of pre-Christian religious life does not represent the fruit of extensive surveys across wide areas, rather it represents the results of a tiny number of minuscule points of contact with pagan religious life. And these points of contact can – particularly when an author as influential as Bede discusses them – become seminal for medieval Christians' understanding of the pre-Christian past. Through these writings, such points of contact can also disproportionately affect our own view of pre-Christian religious life. The treatment of Old Norse mythological narratives centred around the great gods have, as noted in Chapter 1, been a case in point.

The Romano-Germanic votive inscriptions do not provide a quarry from which fragmentary witnesses to the pre-medieval existence of the deities mentioned in medieval sources can, or should, be gathered. However, they do provide a valuable corrective to any sense we may have that the medieval sources provide anything like the full picture. These inscriptions offer us a glimpse of pre-Christian religious life as recorded by the worshippers themselves (or at least by their stone-masons), and it is a glimpse that is chronologically and geographically narrow. This may seem like a disadvantage, but it has advantages over the sparse but broad evidence available in the medieval sources, demonstrating the considerable capacity for regional, local and familial variation even within short timescales and comparatively small areas. At the same time, these inscriptions demonstrate the extent to which pre-Christian religious life was embedded in social and political structures and groupings, and shaped by them – probably much more than it was shaped by notions of specific areas of divine function or expertise.

The many gaps and uncertainties in the evidence discussed here should caution us against believing that we know much about Anglo-Saxon paganism at all. I have tried to demonstrate that there are reasons to believe in the existence of cults of Eostre and Hreda, and that they may well have been two among many. But I would not suggest that these were the only forms of religious life in pre-Christian England, and the arguments put forward above may relate to only one layer in a religious landscape of deities with very different socio-political and geographical patterns of worship. This possibly vast landscape – perhaps a good deal more than half-submerged – still offers many possibilities for exploration, and I hope that this guidebook to one small corner of it may stimulate efforts in other under-explored areas of the terrain.

Notes

1. Cheryl Clay has pointed out to me that some of Birley's etymological identifications have a long history: *Viðrir*, for instance, is mentioned in connection with the *dibus veteribus* by Hodgson (1820-58: vol 3 of part 2, 140), while Bruce (1853: 399) prefers an interpretation as 'the ancient gods'. This is not the place for a complete archaeology of Birley's etymologies, but Birley had already assembled more or less the collection quoted above in his *The People of Roman Britain* (1979: 107-8). Evidently he has been saddled with an etymological collection with substantial roots, and not entirely of his own making.

2. This work is based on data provided through EDINA UKBORDERS with the support of the ESRC and JISC and uses Kain and Oliver historic boundary material which is copyright of the AHDS History [University of Essex], Humphrey Southall, Nick Burton and the University of Portsmouth. The area was calculated from this data using Arcview 3.2.

3. This work is based on data provided through EDINA UKBORDERS with the support of the ESRC and JISC and uses Kain and Oliver historic boundary material which is copyright of the AHDS History [University of Essex], Humphrey Southall, Nick Burton and the University of Portsmouth. The area was calculated from this data using Arcview 3.2.

4. The consistent use of the form *Hild* for the abbess of *Strenaeshalc* in the *Historia Ecclesiastica*, however, does not seem to fit with this pattern (although her name is treated as a first declension noun in the oblique cases), and the names *Begu* and *Heiu*, which occur in book 4, chapter 23, on the life and death of Hild (Plummer 1896: 1.252-8), are also anomalous. Given the evidence for Bede's preservation of name forms from his written sources (Shaw 2008: 102-3), this anomaly may indicate that he had a source relating to Hild's life from which he took these three names.

5. *DOEC* produces 6 matches for the fragmentary sequence <hred> in texts with Cameron numbers beginning 'B15' (i.e. in all charters in *DOEC*), of which only the match in B15.8.295 is certainly an instance of the word *hreod*. In contrast, 36 matches

are produced for the fragmentary sequence <hreod> in texts with Cameron numbers beginning 'B15'.

6. Jones's collation does not appear to be particularly accurate. Comparing Jones's collation of chapter 15 of *De Temporum Ratione* against the digital facsimile of Cologne, Dombibliothek, Cod. 103 (*CEEC*), there are at least twenty cases where Jones fails to note this manuscript's variant, despite the fact that this is one of the manuscripts he claims to have collated in full. To be fair to Jones, many of these missing variants involve ignoring common medieval spelling variants such as <grecorum>, <agustus>, <marcius>, <disperciebant>, <precedit> and <inicium>; but Jones also fails to note a missing *illo*, and does note <nacio> as a variant for *natio*. He is not, then, terribly consistent in what he notes or fails to note, and his inaccuracies also extend to the Old English names included in this chapter. This gives us little grounds for confidence about the spellings of the names *Eostre* and *Hreda* even in the manuscripts he collated, let alone in those he merely examined. I therefore examined chapter fifteen in the following ninth-century manuscripts either in facsimile or in person: Angers, Bibliothèque municipale, 477 (461); Berlin, Staatsbibliothek zu Berlin, Phillipps 1831; Berlin, Staatsbibliothek zu Berlin, Phillipps 1832 (Cat. Rose 130); Berlin, Staatsbibliothek zu Berlin, Phillipps 1869 (Cat. Rose 131); Cambrai, Bibliothèque municipale, 925 (824); Cologne, Dombibliothek, Cod. 83(II) (examined in *CEEC*); Cologne, Dombibliothek, Cod. 102 (examined in *CEEC*); Cologne, Dombibliothek, Cod. 103 (examined in *CEEC*); Geneva, Bibliothèque publique et universitaire, lat. 50; Melk, Bibliothek des Benediktinerstifts, 412 (370. G32); Milan, Biblioteca Ambrosiana, inf. D 30; Paris, Bibliothèque nationale de France, Latin 5543; Paris, Bibliothèque nationale de France, Latin 13013; Paris, Bibliothèque nationale de France, Latin 13403; Paris, Bibliothèque nationale de France, Latin 14088; Paris, Bibliothèque nationale de France, NAL 1632; Rouen, Bibliothèque municipale, I.49 (524); St Gall, Stiftsbibliothek, Cod. Sang. 250 (examined in *CESG*); Valenciennes, Bibliothèque municipale, 174 (166); Valenciennes, Bibliothèque municipale, 343 (330 bis); Vatican, Biblioteca Apostolica Vaticana, Pal. Lat. 1448; Vatican, Biblioteca Apostolica Vaticana, Pal. Lat. 1449. In none of these manuscripts are there any forms of *Hreda* or *Hredmonath* with any vowel in the first syllable other than <e>.

Bibliography

Abbreviations

Bosworth-Toller: Bosworth and Toller 1882.

Bosworth-Toller Supplement: Toller and Campbell 1972.

CEEC: *Codices Electronici Ecclesiae Coloniensis* <http://www.ceec.uni-koeln.de/> [accessed March 2008].

CESG: *Codices Electronici Sangallenses* <http://www.cesg.unifr.ch/> [accessed March 2008].

DOE: *Dictionary of Old English.*

DOEC: Healey, Antonette di Paolo. (ed.). 2004. *Dictionary of Old English Corpus* <http://quod.lib.umich.edu/o/oec/> [accessed August 2008].

Lewis and Short: Lewis and Short 1879.

MED: *Middle English Dictionary.*

PASE: *Prosopography of Anglo-Saxon England* <http://www.pase.ac.uk> [accessed August 2008].

Sawyer: *Anglo-Saxons.net: Charters* <http://www.anglo-saxons.net/hwaet/ ?do=show&page=Charters> [accessed February 2009] (searchable interface to S.E. Kelly, *The Electronic Sawyer* <http://www.trin.cam.ac.uk/chartwww/eSawyer.99/eSawyer2.html> and Sean Miller, *The New Regesta Regum Anglorum* <http://www.trin.cam.ac.uk/chartwww/NewRegReg.html>; individual entries cited by Sawyer number).

References

Abramson, Tony (ed.). 2008. *Two Decades of Discovery*, Studies in Early Medieval Coinage, 1 (Woodbridge: Boydell).

Anderson, Carl Edlund. 1999. *Formation and Resolution of Ideological Contrast in the Early History of Scandinavia* (unpublished doctoral thesis, University of Cambridge) <http://www.carlaz.com/phd/AndersonCE_1999_PhD.pdf> [accessed February 2009].

Bibliography

Anderson, O.S. 1941. *Old English Material in the Leningrad Manuscript of Bede's Ecclesiastical History*, Skrifter Utgivna av Kungl. Humanistiska Vetenskapssamfundet i Lund, 31 (Lund: Gleerup; Leipzig: Harrassowitz; London: Oxford University Press).

Antonsen, Elmer H. 1975. *A Concise Grammar of the Older Runic Inscriptions*, Sprachstrukturen, A3 (Tübingen: Niemeyer).

Ashley, William. 1928. *The Bread of Our Forefathers: An Inquiry into Economic History* (Oxford: Clarendon Press).

Baker, Peter S. 2007. *Introduction to Old English*, 2nd edn (Oxford: Blackwell).

Baker, Peter S. and Lapidge, Michael (eds). 1995. *Byrhtferth's Enchiridion*, Early English Text Society, s.s. 15 (Oxford: Oxford University Press).

Bassett, Steven. 1989a. 'In Search of the Origins of Anglo-Saxon Kingdoms', in Bassett 1989b: 3-27.

Bassett, Steven. 1989b. *The Origins of Anglo-Saxon Kingdoms* (London: Leicester University Press).

Bauchhenß, Gerhard, and Neumann, Günter (eds). 1987. *Matronen und verwandte Gottheiten: Ergebnisse eines Kolloquiums veranstaltet von der Göttinger Akademiekommission für die Altertumskunde Mittel- und Nordeuropas*, Beihefte der Bonner Jahrbücher, 44 (Cologne: Rheinland-Verlag).

Behr, Charlotte. 2000. 'The Origins of Kingship in Early Medieval Kent', *Early Medieval Europe*, 9: 25-52.

Birley, Anthony. 1979. *The People of Roman Britain* (London: Batsford).

Birley, Anthony. 2002. *Garrison Life at Vindolanda: A Band of Brothers* (Stroud: Tempus).

Birley, Eric. 1986. 'The Deities of Roman Britain', in Haase 1986: 3-112.

Blair, John. 1989. 'Frithuwold's Kingdom and the Origins of Surrey', in Bassett 1989b: 97-107.

Blair, Peter Hunter and Mynors, R.A.B. (eds). 1959. *The Moore Bede: Cambridge University Library MS Kk.5.16*, Early English Manuscripts in Facsimile, 9 (Copenhagen: Rosenkilde and Bagger).

Blake, E.O. (ed.). 1962. *Liber Eliensis*, Camden Third Series, 92 (London: Royal Historical Society).

Bosworth, Joseph, and Toller, T. Northcote. 1882. *An Anglo-Saxon Dictionary* (Oxford: Clarendon Press).

Bradley, S.A.J. (ed. and tr.). 1997. *Anglo-Saxon Poetry* (London: Dent).

Brooks, Nicholas. 1989. 'The Creation and Early Structure of the Kingdom of Kent', in Bassett 1989b: 55-74.

Bruce, John Collingwood. 1853. *The Roman Wall: An Historical and Topographical Description of the Barrier of the Lower Isthmus Extending from the Tyne to the Solway*, 2nd edn (London: John Russell Smith).

Cameron, Angus. 1973. 'A List of Old English Texts', in Frank and Cameron 1973: 25-306.

Cameron, Kenneth. 1969. *English Place-Names* (London: Methuen).

Campbell, A. 1959 [1997]. *Old English Grammar* (Oxford: Clarendon Press).

Campbell, Jackson J. 1951. 'The Dialect Vocabulary of the OE Bede', *Journal of English and Germanic Philology*, 50: 349-72.

Campbell, J. 1979. 'Bede's Words for Places', in Sawyer 1979: 34-54.

Carder, David. 2004. 'Anglo-Saxon Churches', in Lawson and Killingray 2004: 31.

Carroll, Maureen. 2001. *Romans, Celts and Germans: The German Provinces of Rome* (Stroud: Tempus).

Cavill, Paul (ed.). 2004. *The Christian Tradition in Anglo-Saxon England: Approaches to Current Scholarship and Teaching* (Cambridge: Brewer).

Chambers, R.W. 1912. *Widsith: A Study in Old English Heroic Legend* (Cambridge: Cambridge University Press).

Clemen, Carl. 1934. *Altgermanische Religionsgeschichte* (Bonn: Röhrscheid).

Clemoes, Peter (ed.). 1997. *Ælfric's Catholic Homilies: The First Series*, Early English Text Society, s.s. 17 (Oxford: Oxford University Press).

Colgrave, Bertram and Mynors, R.A.B. (eds). 1969. *Bede's Ecclesiastical History of the English People* (Oxford: Clarendon Press).

Collingwood, R.G. and Wright, R.P. 1965. *The Roman Inscriptions of Britain, I: Inscriptions on Stone* (Oxford: Clarendon Press).

Cramp, Rosemary. 1984. *Corpus of Anglo-Saxon Stone Sculpture: County Durham and Northumberland*, 2 vols (Oxford: Oxford University Press).

Crawford, O.G.S. 1922. *The Andover District: An Account of Sheet 283 of the One-inch Ordnance Map* (Oxford: Clarendon Press).

Damico, Helen. 1984. *Beowulf's Wealhtheow and the Valkyrie Tradition* (Madison: University of Wisconsin Press).

Davidson, Hilda Ellis. 1972. *The Battle God of the Vikings*, University of York Medieval Monograph Series, 1 (York: University of York).

Davidson, Hilda Ellis. 1998. *Roles of the Northern Goddess* (London: Routledge).

Derks, Ton. 1991. 'The Perception of the Roman Pantheon by a Native Elite: The Example of Votive Inscriptions from Lower Germany', in Roymans and Theuws 1991: 235-65.

Derks, Ton. 1998. *Gods, Temples and Ritual Practices: The Transformation of Religious*

Ideas and Values in Roman Gaul, Amsterdam Archaeological Studies, 2 (Amsterdam: Amsterdam University Press).

De Vries, Jan. 1956-57. *Altgermanische Religionsgeschichte*, 2nd edn, Grundriß der germanischen Philologie, 12, 2 vols (Berlin: de Gruyter).

De Vries, Jan. 1977. *Altnordisches Etymologisches Wörterbuch*, 2nd edn (Leiden: Brill).

DuBois, Thomas A. 1999. *Nordic Religions in the Viking Age* (Philadelphia: University of Pennsylvania Press).

Dumézil, Georges. 1973. *Gods of the Ancient Northmen*, ed. Einar Haugen, tr. John Lindow and others (Berkeley: University of California Press).

Düwel, Klaus (ed.). 1994. *Runische Schriftkultur in kontinental-skandinavischer und -angelsächsischer Wechselbeziehung*, Ergänzungsbände zum Reallexikon der Germanischen Altertumskunde, 10 (Berlin: de Gruyter).

Eis, Gerhard. 1949. *Altdeutsche Handschriften* (Munich: Beck).

Eis, Gerhard. 1964a. 'Deutung des ersten Merseburger Zauberspruchs', in Eis 1964b: 58-66.

Eis, Gerhard. 1964b. *Altdeutsche Zaubersprüche* (Berlin: de Gruyter).

Ekwall, Eilert. 1960. *The Concise Oxford Dictionary of English Place-Names*, 4th edn (Oxford: Clarendon Press).

Feist, Sigmund. 1939. *Vergleichendes Wörterbuch der Gotischen Sprache*, 3rd edn (Leiden: Brill).

Fisher, C.D. (ed.). 1906 [1956]. *Cornelii Taciti Annalium ab Excessu Divi Augusti Libri* (Oxford: Clarendon Press) [unpaginated: cited by book and chapter].

Förster, Max. 1929. 'Die altenglischen Verzeichnisse von Glücks- und Unglückstagen', in Malone and Ruud 1929: 258-77.

Frank, Roberta and Cameron, Angus (eds). 1973. *A Plan for the Dictionary of Old English* (Toronto: University of Toronto Press).

Frings, Theodor and Müller, Gertraud 1966-68. *Germania Romana*, 2nd edn, 2 vols, Mitteldeutsche Studien, 19 (Halle: Niemeyer).

Fulk, R.D. 1992. *A History of Old English Meter* (Philadelphia: University of Pennsylvania Press).

Gallée, J.H. (ed.). 1894. *Old Saxon Texts* (Leiden: Brill).

Gannon, Anna. 2003. *The Iconography of Early Anglo-Saxon Coinage: Sixth to Eighth Centuries* (Oxford: Oxford University Press).

Garman, Alex. G. 2008. *The Cult of the Matronae in the Roman Rhineland: An Historical Evaluation of the Archaeological Evidence* (Lewiston: Mellen).

Gelling, Margaret. 1988. *Signposts to the Past*, 2nd edn (Chichester: Phillimore).

Gerchow, Jan. 1988. *Die Gedenküberlieferung der Angelsachsen*, Arbeiten zur Frühmittelalterforschung, 20 (Berlin: de Gruyter).

Gordon, E.V. and Taylor, A.R. 1957. *An Introduction to Old Norse*, 2nd edn (Oxford: Clarendon Press).

Gradon, P.O.E. (ed.). 1977. *Cynewulf's 'Elene'* (Exeter: University of Exeter).

Green, D.H. 2000. *Language and History in the Early Germanic World* (Cambridge: CUP).

Green, Francis J. 1994. 'Cereals and Plant Food: A Reassessment of the Saxon Economic Evidence from Wessex', in Rackham 1994b: 83-8.

Grimm, Jacob. 1882-88 [1966]. *Teutonic Mythology*, tr. James Steven Stallybrass, 4 vols (New York: Dover).

Gutenbrunner, Siegfried. 1936. *Die germanischen Götternamen der antiken Inschriften*, Rheinische Beiträge und Hülfsbücher zur germanischen Philologie und Volkskunde, 24 (Halle: Niemeyer).

Gutenbrunner, Siegfried. 1966. 'Ostern: Neue Materialen zum Synkretismus der Merowingerzeit', in Rudolph, Heller and Walter 1966: 122-9.

Haase, Wolfgang (ed.). 1986. *Aufstieg und Niedergang der römischen Welt: Geschichte und Kultur Roms im Spiegel der neueren Forschung*, II, 18.1 (Berlin: de Gruyter).

Hammer, Carl I. 1997. *Charlemagne's Months and their Bavarian Labors: The Politics of the Seasons in the Carolingian Empire*, BAR International Series, 676 (Oxford: Archaeopress).

Hawkes, Sonia Chadwick. 1979. 'Eastry in Anglo-Saxon Kent: Its Importance, and a Newly-Found Grave', in Hawkes, Brown and Campbell 1979: 81-113.

Hawkes, Sonia Chadwick, Brown, David and Campbell, James (eds). 1979. *Anglo-Saxon Studies in Archaeology and History* 1, BAR British Series, 72 (Oxford: BAR).

Helm, Karl. 1913-53. *Altgermanische Religionsgeschichte*, 2 vols (Heidelberg: Winter).

Helm, Karl. 1950. 'Erfundene Götter?', in Kienast 1950: 1-11.

Henel, Heinrich. 1934. *Studien zum altenglischen Computus*, Beiträge zur englischen Philologie, 26 (Leipzig: Tauchnitz).

Henel, Heinrich. 1935. 'Altenglischer Mönchsaberglaube', *Englische Studien*, 69: 329-49.

Henel, Heinrich (ed.). 1942 [for 1940]. *Ælfric's De Temporibus Anni*, Early English Text Society, o.s. 213 (London: Oxford University Press).

Herren, Michael W. 1998. 'The Transmission and Reception of Graeco-Roman Mythology in Anglo-Saxon England, 670-800', *Anglo-Saxon England*, 27: 87-103.

Hodgson, John. 1820-58. *History of Northumberland*, 3 parts in 7 vols (Newcastle: the author).

Hofstra, T., Houwen, L.A.J.R. and MacDonald, A.A. (eds). 1995. *Pagans and Christians: The Interplay between Christian Latin and Traditional Germanic Cultures in Early Medieval Europe*, Germania Latina, 2 (Groningen: Forsten).

Hogg, Richard M. 1992. *A Grammar of Old English: Volume 1: Phonology* (Oxford: Blackwell).

Holder-Egger, O. (ed.). 1911. *Einhardi Vita Karoli Magni*, Monumenta Germaniae Historica, Scriptores Rerum Germanicarum in Usum Scholarum, 25 (Hannover: Hahn).

Holthausen, Ferdinand. 1954. *Altsächsisches Wörterbuch*, Niederdeutsche Studien, 1 (Münster: Böhlau).

Hondius-Crone, Ada. 1955. *The Temple of Nehalennia at Domburg* (Amsterdam: Meulenhoff).

Jack, George (ed.). 1994. *Beowulf: A Student Edition* (Oxford: Clarendon Press).

Jeske, Hans. 1983. 'Zu den deutschen Monatsnamen', *Studia Neophilologica*, 55: 31-46.

Jones, Charles W. (ed.). 1943. *Bedae Opera de Temporibus* (Cambridge, MA: The Mediaeval Academy of America).

Jones, Charles W. (ed.). 1977. *Bedae Venerabilis Opera: Pars VI, Opera Didascalica*, 2, Corpus Christianorum, Series Latina, 123 B (Turnhout: Brepols).

Jónsson, Guðni (ed.). 1950. *Fornaldar Sögur Norðurlanda*, 4 vols (Reykjavík: Íslendingasagnaútgáfan).

Kienast, Richard (ed.). 1950. *Studien zur deutschen Philologie des Mittelalters* (Heidelberg: Winter).

Kitson, Peter. 2002. 'Topography, Dialect, and the Relation of Old English Psalter-Glosses (I)', *English Studies*, 83: 474-503.

Kittlick, Wolfgang. 1998. *Die Glossen der Hs. British Library, Cotton Cleopatra A. III: Phonologie, Morphologie, Wortgeographie*, Europäische Hochschulschriften, Reihe 14: Angelsächsische Sprache und Literatur, 347 (Frankfurt: Lang).

Kluge, Friedrich and Seebold, Elmar. 2002. *Etymologisches Wörterbuch der deutschen Sprache*, 24th edn (Berlin: de Gruyter).

Knobloch, Johann. 1959. 'Der Ursprung von nhd. Ostern, engl. Easter', *Die Sprache*, 5: 27-45.

Kolbe, Hans-Georg. 1960. 'Die neuen Matroneninschriften von Morken-Harff, Kreis Bergheim', *Bonner Jahrbücher*, 160: 50-124.

Kölzer, Theo, Hartmann, Martina and Stieldorf, Andrea (eds). 2001. *Die Urkunden der Merowinger*, 2 vols, Monumenta Germaniae Historica: Diplomata Regum Francorum e Stirpe Merovingica (Hannover: Hahn).

Kotzor, Günter (ed.). 1981. *Das altenglische Martyrologium*, Bayerische Akademie der

Wissenschaften, Philosophisch-Historische Klasse, Abhandlungen, Neue Folge, 88, 2 vols (Munich: Verlag der Bayerischen Akademie der Wissenschaften).

Krapp, George Philip (ed.). 1932. *The Vercelli Book*, The Anglo-Saxon Poetic Records, 2 (London: Routledge; New York: Columbia University Press).

Krause, Wolfgang. 1968. *Handbuch des Gotischen*, 3rd edn (Munich: Beck).

Kuhn, Sherman M. (ed.). 1965. *The Vespasian Psalter* (Ann Arbor: University of Michigan Press).

Kuhn, Sherman M. 1972. 'The Authorship of the Old English Bede Revisited', *Neuphilologische Mitteilungen*, 73: 172-80.

Lapidge, Michael et al. (eds). 2001. *The Blackwell Encyclopaedia of Anglo-Saxon England* (Oxford: Blackwell).

Larrington, Carolyne (tr.). 1996. *The Poetic Edda* (Oxford: Oxford University Press).

Lawson, Terence and Killingray, David. 2004. *An Historical Atlas of Kent* (Chichester: Phillimore).

Lawson, Terence. 2004. 'Lathes and Hundreds', in Lawson and Killingray 2004: 30.

Lewis, Charlton T. and Short, Charles 1879 [1998]. *A Latin Dictionary* (Oxford: Clarendon Press).

Liebermann, F. (ed.). 1903-16. *Die Gesetze der Angelsachsen*, 3 vols (Halle: Niemeyer).

Lindelöf, U. (ed.). 1927. *Rituale Ecclesiae Dunelmensis: The Durham Collectar*, Publications of the Surtees Society, 140 (Durham: Andrews).

Lindsay, W.M. (ed.). 1911. *Isidori Hispalensis Episcopi Etymologiarum sive Originum Libri XX*, 2 vols (Oxford: Clarendon Press) [unpaginated: cited by book, chapter and section].

Lindsay, W.M. (ed.). 1921. *The Corpus Glossary* (Cambridge: Cambridge University Press).

Lucas, Peter J. (ed.). 1977. *Exodus* (London: Methuen).

Machan, Tim William (ed.). 2008. *Vafþrúðnismál*, 2nd edn, Durham Medieval and Renaissance Texts, 1 (Toronto: Pontifical Institute of Mediaeval Studies; Durham: Centre for Medieval and Renaissance Studies, Durham University).

Malone, Kemp, and Ruud, Martin B. (eds). 1929. *Studies in Philology: A Miscellany in Honor of Frederick Klaeber* (Minneapolis: University of Minnesota Press).

Marchand, James W. 1973. *The Sounds and Phonemes of Wulfila's Gothic*, Janua Linguarum, Series Practica, 25 (The Hague: Mouton).

McKitterick, Rosamond. 2004. *History and Memory in the Carolingian World* (Cambridge: Cambridge University Press).

McMahon, April and McMahon, Robert. 2005. *Language Classification by Numbers* (Oxford: Oxford University Press).

Bibliography

Meaney, Audrey L. 1979. 'The *Ides* of the Cotton Gnomic Poem', *Medium Ævum*, 48: 23-39.

Meaney, Audrey L. 1985. 'Bede and Anglo-Saxon Paganism', *Parergon*, n.s. 3: 1-29.

Mees, Bernard. 2006. 'Early Rhineland Germanic', *North-Western European Language Evolution*, 49: 13-49.

Meyer, Richard M. 1910. *Altgermanische Religionsgeschichte* (Leipzig: Quelle & Meyer).

Miller, Thomas (ed.). 1890-98. *The Old English Version of Bede's Ecclesiastical History of the English People*, 2 vols, Early English Text Society, o.s. 95, 96, 110, 111 (London: Trübner).

Mills, A.D. 2003. *Oxford Dictionary of British Place-Names* (Oxford: Oxford University Press).

Mommsen, Theodorus (ed.). 1882. *Iordanis Romana et Getica*, Monumenta Germaniae Historica, Auctores Antiquissimi, 5.1 (Berlin: Weidmann).

Muir, Bernard J. 1994. *The Exeter Anthology of Old English Poetry: An Edition of Exeter Dean and Chapter MS 3501*, 2 vols (Exeter: University of Exeter Press).

Murdoch, Brian. 2004a. 'Charms, Recipes, and Prayers', in Murdoch 2004b: 57-72.

Murdoch, Brian (ed.). 2004b. *German Literature of the Early Middle Ages*, The Camden House History of German Literature, 2 (Rochester, NY: Camden House).

Napier, A. 1889. 'Altenglische Kleinigkeiten', *Anglia*, 11: 1-10.

Napier, Arthur S. (ed.). 1900. *Old English Glosses: Chiefly Unpublished*, Anecdota Oxoniensa, Mediaeval and Modern Series, 11 (Oxford: Clarendon Press).

Neumann, Günter. 1987. 'Die germanischen Matronen-Beinamen', in Bauchhenß and Neumann 1987: 103-32.

North, Richard. 1997. *Heathen Gods in Old English Literature*, Cambridge Studies in Anglo-Saxon England, 22 (Cambridge: Cambridge University Press).

Oertel, Kurt. 2003. 'Ostara – eine germanische Göttin?', <http://www.niflungen.de/download/ostara.pdf> [accessed July 2007].

Okasha, Elisabeth. 1971. *Hand-List of Anglo-Saxon Non-Runic Inscriptions* (Cambridge: Cambridge University Press).

Okasha, Elisabeth. 2004. 'Memorial Stones or Grave Stones?', in Cavill 2004: 91-101.

Page, R.I. 1995. 'Anglo-Saxon Paganism: The Evidence of Bede', in Hofstra, Houwen and MacDonald 1995: 99-129.

Petersohn, Jürgen. 1966. 'Neue Bedafragmente in northumbrischer Unziale saec. viii', *Scriptorium*, 20: 215-47.

Peterson, Lena. 1994. 'On the Relationship between Proto-Scandinavian and Continental Germanic Personal Names', in Düwel 1994: 128-75.

Peterson, Lena. 2004. *Lexikon över urnordiska personnamn*, <http://www.sofi.se/1465> [accessed April 2009].

Peterson, Lena. 2007. *Nordiskt runnamnslexikon*, 5th edn (Uppsala: Institutet för språk och folkminnen).

Pheifer, J.D. (ed.). 1974. *Old English Glosses in the Épinal-Erfurt Glossary* (Oxford: Clarendon Press).

Plummer, Carolus. 1896. *Venerabilis Baedae Historiam Ecclesiasticam Gentis Anglorum*, 2 vols (Oxford: Clarendon Press).

Pokorny, Julius. 1959-69. *Indogermanisches etymologisches Wörterbuch*, 2 vols (Bern: Francke).

Rackham, James. 1994a. 'Economy and Environment in Saxon London', in Rackham 1994b: 126-35.

Rackham, James (ed.). 1994b. *Environment and Economy in Anglo-Saxon England: A Review of Recent Work on the Environmental Archaeology of Rural and Urban Anglo-Saxon Settlements in England*, Council for British Archaeology Research Report, 89 (York: Council for British Archaeology).

Reichert, Hermann. 1987-90. *Lexikon der altgermanischen Namen*, Thesaurus Palaeogermanicus, 1, 2 vols (Vienna: Verlag der österreichischen Akademie der Wissenschaften).

Riddler, Ian. 2004. 'Anglo-Saxon Kent: Early Development c. 450-c.800', in Lawson and Killingray 2004: 25-8.

Roeder, Fritz. 1904. *Der altenglische Regius-Psalter: Eine Interlinearversion in Hs. Royal 2. B. 5 des Brit. Mus.*, Studien zur englischen Philologie, 18 (Halle: Niemeyer).

Roffe, David. 1995. 'The Historia Croylandensis: A Plea for Reassessment', *English Historical Review*, 110.435: 93-108.

Roud, Steve. 2006. *The English Year: A Month-by-Month Guide to the Nation's Customs and Festivals, from May Day to Mischief Night* (London: Penguin).

Roymans, N. 1990. *Tribal Societies in Northern Gaul: An Anthropological Perspective*, Cingula, 12 (Amsterdam: Universiteit van Amsterdam).

Roymans, N. and Theuws, F. (eds). 1991. *Images of the Past: Studies on Ancient Societies in Northwestern Europe*, Studies in Pre- en Protohistorie, 7 (Amsterdam: Universiteit van Amsterdam).

Rudolph, Kurt, Heller, Rolf and Walter, Ernst (eds). 1966. *Festschrift Walter Baetke: Dargebracht zu seinem 80. Geburtstage am 28. März 1964* (Weimar: Böhlau).

Rüger, Christoph B. 1987. 'Beobachtungen zu den epigraphischen Belegen der Muttergottheiten in den lateinischen Provinzen des Imperium Romanum', in Bauchhenß and Neumann 1987: 1-30.

Sawyer, P.H. (ed.). 1979. *Names, Words, and Graves: Early Medieval Settlement* (Leeds: School of History, University of Leeds).

Schauerte, Günther. 1987. 'Darstellungen mütterlicher Gottheiten in den römischen Nordwestprovinzen', in Bauchhenß and Neumann 1987: 55-102.

Schützeichel, Rudolf. 2006. *Althochdeutsches Wörterbuch*, 6th edn (Tübingen: Niemeyer)

Scragg, D.G. (ed.). 1992. *The Vercelli Homilies and Related Texts*, Early English Text Society, o.s. 300 (Oxford: Oxford University Press).

Seltén, Bo. 1979. *The Anglo-Saxon Heritage in Middle English Personal Names*, 2 vols (Lund: Gleerup).

Sermon, Richard. 2008. 'From Easter to Ostara: The Reinvention of a Pagan Goddess?', *Time and Mind: The Journal of Archaeology, Consciousness and Culture*, 1.3: 331-43.

Shaw, Philip. 2007. 'The Origins of the Theophoric Week in the Germanic Languages', *Early Medieval Europe*, 15: 386-401.

Shaw, Philip. 2008. 'Orthographic Standardization and Seventh- and Eighth-Century Coin Inscriptions', in Abramson 2008: 97-112.

Simek, Rudolf. 1993 [2000]. *Dictionary of Northern Mythology*, tr. Angela Hall (Cambridge: Brewer).

Simek, Rudolf. 2002. 'Goddesses, Mothers, Dísir: Iconography and Interpretation of the Female Deity in Scandinavia in the First Millennium', in Simek and Heizmann 2002: 93-123.

Simek, Rudolf, and Heizmann, Wilhelm (eds). 2002. *Mythological Women: Studies in Memory of Lotte Motz, 1922-1997*, Studia Medievalia Septentionalia, 7 (Vienna: Fassbaender).

Smith, A.H. 1931. 'Þeodric in "Widsith" and the Rök Inscription', *Modern Language Review*, 26: 330-2.

Smith, A.H. 1956. *English Place-Name Elements*, 2 vols, English Place-Name Society, 25-6 (Cambridge: Cambridge University Press).

Spence, Lewis. 1979. *The Minor Traditions of British Mythology* (New York: Arno).

Stevenson, Joseph, and George Waring (eds). 1854-65. *The Lindisfarne and Rushworth Gospels*, 4 vols, Publications of the Surtees Society, 28, 39, 43, 48 (Durham: Andrews).

Stolte, B.H. 1986. 'Die religiösen Verhältnisse in Niedergermanien', in Haase 1986: 591-671.

Ström, Hilmer. 1939. *Old English Personal Names in Bede's History: An Etymological-Phonological Investigation*, Lund Studies in English, 8 (Lund: Gleerup).

Stuart, P. 2003. *Nehalennia: Documenten in Steen* (Goes: De Koperen Tuin).

Stuart, P. and Bogaers, J.E. 2001. *Nehalennia: Römische Steindenkmäler aus der*

Oosterschelde bei Colijnsplaat, Corpus Signorum Imperii Romani, Nederland, 2, 2 vols (Leiden: Rijksmuseum van Oudheden).

Sweet, Henry (ed.). 1885 [1957]. *The Oldest English Texts*, Early English Text Society, o.s. 83 (London: Oxford University Press).

Tangl, Michael. 1916. *Die Briefe des Heiligen Bonifatius und Lullus*, Monumenta Germaniae Historica, Epistolae Selectae, 1 (Berlin: Weidmann).

Toller, T. Northcote, and Campbell, Alistair. 1972. *An Anglo-Saxon Dictionary: Supplement, with Revised and Enlarged Addenda* (Oxford: Oxford University Press).

Toon, Thomas E. 1983. *The Politics of Early Old English Sound Change* (New York: Academic Press).

Udolph, Jürgen. 1999. *Ostern: Geschichte eines Wortes*, Indogermanische Bibliothek: Reihe 3, Untersuchungen, 20 (Heidelberg: Winter).

van Els, T.J.M. 1972. *The Kassel Manuscript of Bede's 'Historia Ecclesiastica Gentis Anglorum' and its Old English Material* (Assen: Van Gorcum).

Wallis, Faith (tr.). 1999. *Bede: The Reckoning of Time*, Translated Texts for Historians, 29 (Liverpool: Liverpool University Press).

Wartmann, Hermann (ed.). 1981. *Urkundenbuch der Abtei Sanct Gallen*, 2 vols (Frankfurt am Main: Minerva Verlag).

Weinhold, Karl. 1869. *Die deutschen Monatnamen* (Halle: Waisenhaus).

Wessén, Elias. 1958. *Runstenen vid Röks Kyrka*, Kungl. Vitterhets Historie och Antikvitets Akademiens Handlingar, Filologisk-Filosofiska Serien, 5 (Stockholm: Almqvist & Wiksell).

Whitelock, Dorothy. 1962. 'The Old English Bede', *Proceedings of the British Academy*, 48: 57-90.

Wilson, H.A. (ed.) 1896. *The Missal of Robert of Jumièges*, Henry Bradshaw Society, 11 (London: Henry Bradshaw Society).

Wolfram, Herwig. 1990. *History of the Goths*, tr. Thomas J. Dunlap (Berkeley: University of California Press).

Wormald, Francis (ed.) 1934. *English Kalendars Before A.D. 1100*, Henry Bradshaw Society, 72 (London: Henry Bradshaw Society).

Wright, Joseph. 1924. *Grammar of the Gothic Language* (Oxford: Clarendon Press).

Index of Words

Index of Words

Old High German

gau, 68
hradi/redi, 95
hriot, 74
itis, 61-3
lentzinmanoth, 95
ôst, 56
ôstar, 51, 58
ôstarmânoth, 51, 95
ôstarun, 50-1, 53-4, 61, 95
ruod, 78

Old Norse

austr, 51, 56-8
bein, 91
dagr, 58
dísir, 61-3

eitr, 58
hraðr, 86
hreið, 86, 91, 93-4
Hreiðgotar, *see* Reiðgotar
hróðr, 80, 86
hveðrung, 15-16
hvítr, 15-16
páskir, 51-2
Reiðgotaland, 90
Reiðgotar, 90-1
þing, 38

Old Saxon

hriod, 74
idis, 61-3
ôst, 56

General Index

126